THE ESSENTIAL
QUIT®
GUIDE TO
STOPPING
SMOKING

GW00696037

THE ESSENTIAL
QUIT®
GUIDE TO
STOPPING
SMOKING

Sarah Litvinoff

coronet

CORONET BOOKS
Hodder & Stoughton

First published in Great Britain in 2001 by Hodder and Stoughton
A division of Hodder Headline

A Coronet Paperback

10 9 8 7 6 5 4 3 2 1

British Library Cataloguing in Publication Data
Litvinoff, Sarah
The essential QUIT guide to stopping smoking
1. Smoking cessation programs
I. Title II. QUIT
613.8′5

ISBN 0 340 76896 7

Typeset by Palimpsest Book Production Limited,
Polmont, Stirlingshire
Printed and bound in Great Britain by
Mackays of Chatham PLC, Chatham, Kent

Hodder and Stoughton
A division of Hodder Headline
338 Euston Road
London NW1 3BH

Acknowledgements

Many people at QUIT contributed their expertise to this book. QUITLINE counsellors in particular generously supplied much of the technical knowledge and practical assistance gained from their training, and the experience of working at the front line with people who seek help in giving up smoking. They are warm, dedicated, humorous, innovative and sympathetic. Bridget Gardiner, the Director of Fundraising at QUIT, efficiently nurtured the project from start to finish, and Peter McCabe, the Chief Executive, whose vision the book was, ensured that it maintained the standards for which QUIT is noted. Other experts involved include Dr Jonathan Foulds, Director, University of Medicine and Dentistry of New Jersey Tobacco Dependency Programme, and Gay Sutherland, Honorary Consultant Clinical Psychologist at the Tobacco Research Section, National Addiction Centre, Institute of Psychiatry (King's College London).

Sarah Litvinoff would particularly like to thank Laura Marcus, who stepped in to research and draft at a difficult time, with her usual speedy professionalism. She was a constant support, resource and good friend – inspiringly cheerful and unflustered. Thanks also go to everyone who shared their experiences of giving up smoking: Vida Adamoli, Louise Baker, Jim Cochrane, Niki Cooper, Lorraine Hindes, Susan Hughes, Dorothy Jantschewsky, Emanuel Litvinoff, Cherry Marshall, George Metcalfe, Tessa Souter, Karen Sullivan and John Waterhouse, as well as others who contributed their stories anonymously, including many QUITLINE counsellors, Quitters of the Year, and callers to QUITLINE.

Contents

Introduction   1

1: Thinking about stopping   7
   What's stopping you stopping? 10; The good news
   about quitting 19; The good news about relapsing
   20; The myths that stop you stopping 23; *I need
   willpower and I don't have enough of it* 23; *If I
   give up smoking I'll get fat* 24; *Smoking helps me
   to cope with stress* 26; Tough stuff – the bad news
   about smoking 29; Heart and circulation 29; Cancer
   30; Respiratory disease 30; Sex and fertility 31;
   Smoking and pregnancy 32; Your looks 33; Are you
   ready to quit? 34

2: Preparing to stop   37
   Setting a date 40; Cutting down or giving up
   completely? 43; Planning your quitting strategy 44;
   The power of habit 45; Strategies to help as you
   break the habit 47; 50 ways to beat your habit 48;
   Strategies to help deal with situations in which you

are tempted to smoke 52; Strategies to help deal
with emotions 53; *I most need to smoke when I'm
under stress* 55; *I most need to smoke when I'm
bored* 58; *I most need to smoke when I'm angry
or irritable* 59; *I most need to smoke when I'm
nervous* 61; *I most need to smoke when I'm lonely*
62; *I most need to smoke when I want a treat* 63;
I most need to smoke when I'm having fun 64; *I
most need to smoke when I hate myself* 65; *I most
need to smoke when I want to rebel* 67; Finding
people to support you 69; Dealing with people who
don't want you to succeed 73; Projects that will
increase your resolve 76

3: Stopping   81

Make a date and stick to it 82; Stopping on impulse
84; Enforced quitting 85; Keep busy 88; Drink lots
of fluid 89; Get more active 90; Ten ways to get
more exercise into your life 92; Think positively
92; Change your routine 95; No excuses 102; Treat
yourself 104; Be careful what you eat 106; Take one
day at a time 107

4: Coping with withdrawal   109

The three kinds of withdrawal 113; Living without
nicotine: physical withdrawal 114; How nicotine
affects your brain 115; What withdrawal feels

like 117; Physical symptoms 118; Psychological
and emotional symptoms of withdrawal 122;
Withdrawing from the habit 126

5: Staying stopped   **129**
When being a non-smoker becomes normal 132;
Dealing with emotions and trigger situations 136;
Stress 137; Ten ways to counteract stress 138;
Uncomfortable emotions 141; Anger 142; Feeling
deprived 144; Social pressure 146; Putting on
weight 147; Dealing with a relapse 150; Successful
quitters 152

6: Being a support – helping a smoker to quit   **155**
Before they are ready 157; Living with a smoker
163; Supporting a quitter 163; Supporting long
term 166; Supporting a quitter who has relapsed
167; Supporting a quitter when you still smoke
yourself 168; When they are tempted to smoke 170;
Do you really want them to succeed? 170; Quitting
together 170

**7: What works? How to find the quitting method
that works for you**   **173**
Nicotine Replacement Therapy (NRT) 176;
Which method of NRT will work best for you?

177; Nicotine gum 177; Nicotine lozenges 179;
Nicotine tablets 179; Nicotine patches 180;
Inhalator 182; Nasal spray 182; When NRT might
not be appropriate 183; Zyban 184; Non-nicotine
products 185; Capsules 185; Dummy cigarettes 185;
Herbal cigarettes 185; Filters 188; Mouthwash 187;
Counselling and support groups 187; QUITLINE
187; Counselling 188; Life Coaching 188; Internet
support 189; Smoker's Clinics 189; Alternative
Therapies 190; Hypnosis and hypnotherapy 190;
Acupuncture 191; Laser therapy 192; Homeopathy
192; Allen Carr Method 192; Conclusion 194

Further Help   **195**

Index   **197**

Introduction

This book has grown out of QUIT's unrivalled knowledge of the help and support people need to give up smoking. QUITLINE (0800 002200), our telephone helpline, has talked to over two million would-be ex-smokers and those in the process of giving up, making it the busiest smoking cessation support system anywhere in the world, and it is completely free to those using it.

What the QUITLINE counsellors have learned through helping millions towards their goal is that there is no such thing as an average smoker and no 'best way' to give up smoking. There are many reasons why people light up their first cigarette, and many more complex reasons why they continue smoking, despite knowing the health dangers, despite the nagging or disapproval of others, and despite – in most cases – a real desire to stop. Addiction to nicotine is only part of it: the act of smoking has an emotional and psychological effect, and it is also a habit.

QUITLINE counsellors are trained to unravel what it is that each caller derives from smoking, and what is stopping that individual from quitting when he or she wants to so much. Callers are often surprised not to get a health lecture, as they might from some health professionals. QUITLINE will give such information if asked – all counsellors have completed the QUIT Certification in Smoking Cessation and Telephone Counselling, in which leading experts advise on all aspects of smoking and addiction – but QUIT knows that for most people positive encouragement is much more effective than scare-mongering. Counsellors work with callers to design a plan best suited to the individual's personality, needs and circumstances.

In this book, the same applies. There is information about the health implications of smoking, for those of you who find it helps your resolve, but it is far out-weighed by the range of tried and tested positive tips and suggestions, and objective analyses of the products and services that have helped some people to quit. You'll hear the true stories of dozens of successful quitters, and eavesdrop on QUITLINE counsellors' conversations with people at various stages of progress. If you're concerned about someone else's smoking you'll find out the best way to support them through the process of giving up.

QUIT's credentials stretch back to 1926, when it was first formed by a group including many doctors, and was known as the National Society of Non-Smokers. These pioneers were passionately anti-smoking at a time when the health implications were not as well understood as they are today, and some of the founder members were known to throw buckets of water over hapless smokers in the street. The name change to QUIT in 1989 reflected the fact that the emphasis for the group had changed – the charity began to focus on providing practical support and help for quitters, rather than on campaigning for tobacco control, which was being carried out to high standards by the sister organisation: Action on Smoking and Health (ASH).

QUIT pursues its aims in a number of ways. It launched 'Break Free' in 1994 to encourage young people not to start smoking and to offer specialised help to those wanting to quit. This targets the 30 percent of teenagers who smoke, and especially the 67 percent in the 16 to 19 age group who have made an unsuccessful attempt to quit. The need for targeted help for teenagers is shown by the fact that 74 percent of adult smokers began before they were 18 years old.

The QUIT schools programme offers presentations to 11 to 18 year olds on the dangers of smoking and also recognises the very real pressures many teenagers experience from friends who smoke. There's no lecturing or preaching, simply a wealth of information to make an informed choice about smoking.

QUIT also targets people on low incomes or benefits who spend a disproportionately large share of their income on cigarettes and smoke more than the general population. QUIT helps low-income smokers in two ways: a community advice programme recruits and trains ex-smokers from low-income communities to run their own local smoking cessation groups and to act as role models, and a Social Worker and Money

Adviser training programme is available for professionals who are in regular contact with low-income smokers.

At the other end of the scale, Quit has worked with well over 1000 companies that are instituting no-smoking policies, running courses and workshops for employees who want to break the habit for good.

The expertise from these various activities culminates in Quitline. Counsellors talk to people aged from eight to eighty, from stressed executives to people on benefits. Callers include those who have stopped but need help to remain ex-smokers. A significant number of children and teenagers ring for help to stop, or because they are worried about someone they love who smokes.

Quit also recognised that certain communities need specialised help. The Asian Quitline, launched in 1997, offers counselling in five Asian languages – Bengali, Gujerati, Hindi, Punjabi and Urdu – with advice appropriate to the caller's culture. Turkish/Kurdish Quitline started in 1999. The Pregnancy Quitline is a support for the three-quarters of women in the UK who continue to smoke during their pregnancy, affecting their health and that of their unborn children. It offers an intensive programme of telephone support for women who want to stop smoking – helping them quit, and remain smoke-free beyond the birth of their babies.

What happens when you call Quitline?

You will be put through to a trained counsellor who will answer any questions you have, and work with you on whatever is concerning you: whether you are wondering if you could even contemplate giving up, are trying to strengthen your resolve, have already stopped for a while, or have had a set-back and have started smoking again. The counsellors, who come from many different cultures and backgrounds, are there to help, not to judge, and no one will attempt to persuade, coerce or frighten you; many are ex-smokers themselves, who might have tried and failed more than once before finally giving up.

You can call QUITLINE as often as you like during the opening hours, and for as long as you need support through the process of giving up. You'll rarely get the same counsellor again, which means that you'll have the benefit of a wide range of tips and strategies each time you call. The calls are completely confidential. Children, particularly, might find it helpful to know that no one will be told about their call, not even their parents, and the call will not appear on the telephone bill.

Most of the time you spend on the telephone with a counsellor is designed to help you to make the decision to give up for yourself, and to work out the strategies that would be most useful for you, given your individual circumstances. As one counsellor said, 'I get you to look at what the decision to stop means to you, and to acknowledge that it's something you've chosen. Together we then try to find ways to remind you constantly that it's your choice whether you smoke or not – which puts you in control. Most people say, "I haven't got any willpower". But you can create it and that's the nature of what we're trying to do – help you create your own willpower. Willpower is not about being strong it's about strategising, so you don't have to call on it.'

This book offers the tools you need to develop your own strategy. Dip into it, take what's most useful to you, use it to support you – whether this is your first attempt to give up or your umpteenth. Practice helps you become better at whatever it is you set out to do, and giving up smoking is no exception.

Chapter One

Thinking about stopping

Giving up smoking is not easy, or there would be no need for QUITLINE (0800 002200), or for books like this. But, in essence, it is simple: make up your mind not to take another puff. If you really want to give up you will.

There are many methods available to help you quit – from products and treatments you pay for, to freely available hints and strategies that have helped others – and all are described in this book. But, as our counsellors have found, there is no magic, sure-fire method that works for everyone.

When you are truly ready to stop, any method might help and, when you're not ready, no method will. Even some of the most apparently addicted smokers have given up 'cold turkey' – which means giving up using no special help at all – when they are finally ready.

That readiness may come in a flash: someone you know is diagnosed with a serious illness, or you are. Or perhaps something apparently unimportant that you see or hear clicks with you in a profound way, and you know that you will never smoke again.

For other people it takes years to be ready. Years of worrying, thinking about it, talking about it, perhaps half-hearted or failed attempts to give up, until one day they are sure. According to numerous surveys over a number of years, 70 percent of adult smokers would like to stop. Some people are surprised to find that when they finally are resolved to quit, they are able to do so without any of the difficulties they have expected, or have encountered before. But when you are truly resolved, it will carry you through many of the difficulties that you do have. This chapter can help you think through what smoking means to you, and to find your own resolve within it.

ACTION Your Quit notebook. Buy yourself a notebook that you will use as you start the process of quitting. It will act as your support as you go through the stages. There are a number of suggested written exercises throughout this book which you can complete in your notebook, and which will serve as a spur and reminder as you progress. Feel free to do or not do any of the suggested exercises, and to accept or reject any of the hints. Aim to build up your own unique guide to quitting – doing it your way, for yourself and for your own reasons, is the secret of success.

I didn't start smoking till I was twenty, when everyone smoked. I tried it to see what the fuss was about. But after six years, the

media pressure on the ill effects got to me. So I tried to stop. I
went for acupuncture but I needed a fag for the pain. Then I tried
hypnotism. That didn't work. I'm a typical type A personality – like
to be in control, worry a lot, quick to anger, not at all laid back.
Type As tend not to respond to relaxation therapy or hypnosis.
And I had a high tolerance of smoking: it never made me ill even
though I smoked up to 40 a day. Fewer people were smoking and
instead of just lighting up in someone's house I'd ask if it was all
right. Then I met my girlfriend, who was an ex-smoker. She hated
me smoking but that only made it worse. A few years later, I broke
my leg and I started jogging once it mended to get it going again.
My desire to smoke fizzled out as the running bug bit. I bought
all the gear and entered a race. I was terrified of coming last so
I stopped smoking the week before and haven't had or wanted
one since. That was six years ago. I never had any cravings or
withdrawal symptoms.

This chapter helps you to think about stopping in three
main ways. First of all, you need to understand what is
stopping you stopping. What is it about smoking that is so
pleasurable or necessary to you, and therefore likely to get
in the way of your good intentions? Then you need to know
why it is you want to stop – by no means the same reasons for
everyone. Finally, you need to assess whether you are ready.

You will be ready to stop when your reasons for stopping become stronger than your reasons for continuing. This
strengthens your resolve. You are ready to quit when the
circumstances are right, so that you can turn the resolve to
quit into positive action.

I was only a social smoker, but it took me ages to make up my mind to stop – precisely for that reason. I told myself it wasn't a problem; I wasn't addicted. Then I moved to the stage of asking myself, 'What am I getting from this?' and it wasn't an awful lot. It was only in my late thirties that I finally thought, 'There's no point in this.' Only then did I start questioning the health side of it, because I noticed that every time I did smoke socially it wasn't just the one. My voice was croaky, I had a terrible taste in my mouth the next morning – and there were two cancers of the throat in my family. It was then I thought, 'I really can't ignore that.' Having clarified that, it wasn't a problem to stop, but I had to get to that point first. The time's got to be right.

What's stopping you stopping?

One of the first questions a QUITLINE counsellor is likely to ask is: *what do you get out of smoking?* Some people don't know the answer. They might say simply, 'I need to – I have to smoke', or 'I just do it. I've been doing it since I was 12'. They blame the addiction to nicotine. Other people are very clear about what smoking does for them, or it becomes clearer as they answer the counsellor's questions.

The reasons are often complex. Addiction is part of it: the need for another hit of nicotine causes you to light up. There is also the habitual side. You pick up a cigarette without even thinking, or certain situations make you reach for one: after a meal, when drinking with friends and so on. Beyond this there is the psychological or emotional attachment you have to smoking. Many people describe it as a friend, who is always there when you are sad, angry, bored or want to reward yourself, or as an aid to making a difficult phone call. Or it may be a bonding ritual with other smokers, at parties or outside the office; you prefer the company of smokers.

Some people believe it helps them to cope with stress or to keep their weight down, and some think it helps with concentration at work.

For many younger smokers it's about belonging. All their friends smoke, and it's considered cool to do so. Perhaps it's considered wimpish or goody-goody to stop. It can make them feel grown up, or offers a way of rebelling against adults.

CALLER (very young girl, pretending to be older) I smoke 60 cigarettes a day!

QUITLINE That's a lot for your age!

CALLER Yes. I've been trying to give up but I'm having extreme difficulty because I'm stressed out because my husband's sleeping with someone else.

QUITLINE (teasing) Blimey, you sound far too young to be married.

CALLER (laughs and starts to talk normally) I was just pretending. I do want to stop, but all my friends smoke and they wouldn't want to be friends with me if I didn't.

QUITLINE How long have you all been friends?

CALLER Oh, years and years.

QUITLINE So you were friends before you started smoking. And they liked you then, so it's not just because you smoke. Have you actually mentioned that you'd like to stop?

CALLER Yes, but they all laugh at me.

QUITLINE So you're the one with the brains in the group.

Some people may be surprised to hear that rebellion can also be a factor in later life – sometimes the only act of a rebellion in an otherwise steady and ordered life. What activates this rebellious streak is often other people nagging you to stop smoking – or even reading about the ill-effects. For this reason, 'No Smoking Day' is a spur for some people to smoke even more than usual.

CALLER I've cut right down to five a day. But I just can't give up those. No one knows I smoke – especially not the kids, I go outside to have them. Then I clean my teeth and wash my hands.

QUITLINE What is it about those cigarettes that you enjoy so much?

CALLER I look forward to them. They're my reward. I suppose I also like them being secret; they're something just for me.

QUITLINE Perhaps it could help to find another way of rewarding yourself.

CALLER I suppose so. My husband's away a lot, and the evenings drag. That's when I most crave them.

QUITLINE It sounds as if cigarettes feel like a companion.

CALLER That's exactly right. I feel lonely a lot of the time.

QUITLINE So they're helping you through an emotional experience?

CALLER Yes; I hadn't thought of it like that.

QUITLINE It's important to recognise your ambivalence: part of you wants to stop, but part of you enjoys it. It helps to see what that part enjoys about smoking, and find other ways of dealing with the emotional side. (*They went on to discuss strategies for doing this.*)

Knowing what you get from smoking is one of the keys to successful stopping.

ACTION Think about why you smoke, and in your notebook list the reasons you find it pleasurable or necessary.

Observe yourself
If you're not sure what it is you enjoy about smoking, or when it is you feel most in need, spend a day or two observing yourself.

ACTION Whenever you light up a cigarette, note the time you do so and what is prompting you. Why do you want it now? What's going on? What are you feeling? If you wish, you can also ask yourself whether you really want it and whether you are enjoying it. Some people find that sometimes they smoke as a reflex action, whereas at other times it is much more important to them. You will discover which cigarettes appear to be most essential, which will give you important information about what aspect of quitting will be hardest for you.

Why do you want to stop?
This might seem a strange question. Indeed, sometimes when QUITLINE counsellors ask it callers become annoyed or

think they are crazy. 'Well, it's bad for me, isn't it?' is a typical response. In fact, although the very real dangers to health are a motivating factor for many people, particularly as they grow older, for others there are different reasons that seem more compelling.

My parents smoked heavily and I remember thinking as a kid, 'I can't wait to smoke!' By the age of 13, I was nicking theirs and by 14, I was buying my own. Not everyone in my class smoked but all the kids I wanted to be like did. Doling out fags was a great short cut to popularity. I never worried about lung cancer, even after they started printing warnings on the packets. I remember my mum blowing derisory smoke over them. But by the time I hit my mid-twenties, I noticed that every time I got a cold, it went straight on to my chest. I'd always give up then, till I got better. Apart from that, I made several attempts to stop and occasionally succeeded for a few months. I thought I could be an occasional smoker but I couldn't. I liked it too much. Then I got a really bad cold. I lost my voice which was serious. I was a news reporter and had to cover a general election count and phone the result over to ITN. It was the first time I'd covered a general election and it should have been exciting but it wasn't. I could barely speak. I'll never forget how awful I felt. I vowed never to smoke again. That was on 11 June 1983, the year of the massive Tory landslide. But the politics passed me by – that night signified the day cigarettes finally lost their hold over me.

For some people a great motivating factor is money. Smoking is unquestionably expensive, and becomes more so with every budget. You'll notice that in this book we don't mention prices, because they will be out of date before it is even in the shops – one thing you can count on is that the price will continue to rise. Anyone who stops smoking, however little they smoke, will be substantially better off in a relatively short time.

Other reasons for quitting include the fact that it is increasingly frowned on by other people and often considered to be socially unacceptable. Some people mind what it does to their appearance: ageing the skin, staining the teeth, or the fact that it makes their clothes and hair smell, or that they taste bad when kissing.

YOUNG CALLER I don't know what to do. This boy has asked me out, but he doesn't smoke and he says he wants me to stop, but I don't think I can give up.

QUITLINE Is he drop-dead gorgeous?

CALLER Yes!

QUITLINE What kind of contest is that? Between drop-dead gorgeous and some little white things in a packet?

You might worry about what passive smoking is doing to your children, or not want them to become smokers like you. Many women feel impelled to give up when they become pregnant because of the damage they are doing to their unborn child.

CALLER I'm three months pregnant and I can't stop smoking. Everyone tells me that I'm doing my baby terrible damage, and I know it, but I just can't help myself!

QUITLINE You sound as if you're under a lot of pressure.

CALLER Well, of course I am. Every single cigarette is affecting my baby. I'm desperate to stop, but I can't use patches because the nicotine is no good for the baby.

QUITLINE The guilt you're feeling and the pressure you're under are actually making it harder for you.

CALLER How can I not feel guilty? I've already hurt my baby!

QUITLINE Forget about what you've done up until now. The moment you stop your baby feels the benefit.

CALLER That's reassuring. But I've tried to give up loads of times, and I can't.

QUITLINE You've talked about giving up for the baby. Wouldn't you also feel better about yourself if you stopped?

CALLER I wouldn't be so worried about my own health. I'd feel really good that I'd done something I'd set out to do. I'd feel more confident in myself. (*They talked about ways she could cope with the craving.*)

CALLER Thank you. I feel much more positive. It's made a difference talking about what I can do for the best rather than what I've already done for the worst.

Other women want to quit because they'd like to have children, and smoking is affecting their fertility. Men may be motivated by the fact that smoking reduces the blood flow to the penis, thus putting them at risk of impotence. Both men and women may mind that they are becoming shorter of breath, so aren't as good at sports as they were. Similarly, some singers or actors worry about what it is doing to their voice or their breath control. Others resent the addiction, and not being in charge of their own lives.

CALLER Last weekend my boyfriend and I stayed with friends before a wedding. There were three other couples, and we were the only ones who smoked. We sat away from the others, and tried to blow our smoke away from them. Nobody said anything to make us feel bad, but I felt awful because I felt I had no choice in the matter. I would have liked the option not to smoke, but I had to.

QUITLINE It sounds as if at the moment cigarettes are controlling your life.

CALLER That's what it feels like. Whether I'm on a plane or a train or at work, all I'm thinking about is where and when my next cigarette is going to be.

QUITLINE Giving up is like taking control of your life. It's empowering.

CALLER Yes, they *are* controlling me, it's about time I turned the tables.

There are no good or bad reasons for stopping. The best reason is the one that motivates you. Nobody can tell you why you should quit, or why you should want to. This is why the weakest reason is stopping for someone else, or because someone else tells you to. When this is your main reason, relapsing is much more likely. QUIT counsellors always check that you have your own compelling reasons for quitting, or help you to find them if it appears you are just giving up to please another person.

ACTION List in your notebook all the reasons you want to stop. This is a list you may want to return to time and again when your resolve needs strengthening. It is also useful to make a copy that you carry around with you and can look at often throughout the day. Putting it in your wallet is ideal. Start each sentence with the words, 'I want to stop smoking because . . .' Using the word 'want' puts you in touch with your real desires. Do not write, 'I ought' or 'I should'. These words indicate that that they are not your own reasons – and stopping smoking for reasons that are not truly your own rarely works.

As you consider your reasons for wanting to stop, you will probably start to think of life beyond smoking. How will life be different, in a good way, when you are free from the need to smoke? What will you do with the money that you save? What will it be like not to gauge every situation for when and how you will be able to smoke? How will it feel to be free from having to dash out late at night because you are running low on supplies? How much better will you feel around non-smokers and children?

ACTION Make a list of the ways your life will improve when you no longer need to smoke. What will the advantages be? As well as long-term health benefits, think about your daily life and how different you'll feel without this dependency.

If you are finding it hard to come up with reasons for any of your lists, the following might help you.

The good news about quitting

The benefits start to mount up from the moment you give up smoking. You'll have more money in your pocket. You won't smell of tobacco smoke. Your options won't be limited by whether and where you can smoke. Even better news is that your body starts to recover immediately from the harmful effects of smoking.

- After 20 minutes: Your blood pressure and pulse rate begin to return to normal. The circulation in your hands and feet will also begin to improve.
- After 24 hours: Nicotine has left your body. Your lungs start to clear out mucus and other debris.
- After 48 hours: Carbon monoxide gas is eliminated from your body. Your ability to taste and smell improves.
- After 72 hours: Breathing becomes easier as your bronchial tubes relax. Your energy levels increase.
- After 2 to 12 weeks: Circulation improves, making walking easier.
- After 3 to 9 months: Breathing problems, such as coughing and shortness of breath, improve. Overall lung function can improve by 5–10 percent. Many smokers report feeling less stressed than when they were smoking.
- After 1 year: Risk of coronary heart disease is halved,

and over the next 15 years falls more gradually to that of a non-smoker.

- After 10 years: The risk of lung cancer falls by 30–50 percent and continues to fall thereafter. As an ex-smoker you now have nearly as little risk of developing lung cancer as someone who has never smoked.

The good news about relapsing

Some people decide to give up smoking and do just that – they stop and never start again. But many would-be non-smokers give up and restart a number of times before they finally quit for good.

Most people regard this as failure. They believe they are weak-willed or that their addiction is just too strong. They feel they are doomed to be smokers for the rest of their lives. The truth is different. Every time you make the attempt to give up smoking you learn more about yourself and your habit. You discover the particular triggers that cause you to relapse. Whether it's stress, anxiety, a deadline to meet, or a what-the-hell attitude when you are having a particularly good time, this information can be used to your advantage at your next attempt. Knowing your areas of vulnerability makes you better able to plan for these eventualities in the future.

CALLER I've tried to give up before, but I've never managed it. The longest was for two weeks on holiday, but as soon as I got back I started again. I failed badly.

QUITLINE But that's a success. You're learning how to give up

– and you managed to do so for two weeks. Congratulations! It's a difficult challenge, and like any challenge you get better at it the more you try and the more you learn – then you'll eventually succeed.

Relapsing is part of succeeding

Relapsing can be part of the giving-up process, though hundreds of people manage to stop first time. It takes time to become good at anything that is worth doing, and becoming a non-smoker is no exception. Each attempt to give up is practice for the real thing. The practice increases your chance of success next time.

ACTION Think back to your previous attempts to give up smoking, and what happened to make you start again. List the reasons in your notebook. When you are next ready to give up you can use this knowledge to prepare for similar things happening in the future, and devise strategies to deal with them.

What relapsing teaches you

When you go back to smoking you test your resolve. Were your reasons for quitting compelling enough? Were you doing it for yourself, or to please someone else? Are you experiencing an emotional situation for which smoking has been your only solution in the past? Are you experiencing cravings? The answers to these kinds of questions tell you what needs fixing for the next time.

Giving up smoking is a life change. Like any major change you make, such as moving house, getting married, or even going away on holiday, it is initially stressful, and it takes time to adjust. The act of stopping smoking is just the start. The change to becoming a fully fledged non-smoker happens over a period of time. You'll do it at your own rate. For the lucky ones it is quick and easy. For the rest it is more difficult and, at certain times, that difficulty increases. For a few, the desire to smoke may occasionally return at times, even years later, but if your reasons for quitting are strong enough, it is just a momentary temptation that is easy to resist.

I smoked most when I went out with friends – 20 in an evening. I never smoked in the morning. I stopped before I had my first child, and didn't smoke for years. But then, having dinner with friends, I'd see someone smoking and think 'That'd be nice!' and have the odd one. And the next day! My mouth would taste disgusting! I went through cycles when my smoking would creep up and then I'd stop again. I haven't smoked for six or seven years but even now in that situation I think I'd love one, and I think – I wish they didn't smell so bad, and taste so bad, and weren't so bad for you, because I'd really like to have one. It just is a very social thing to do.

For many people, however, eventually the idea of smoking becomes unthinkable.

I gave up smoking fifteen years ago. I had become vegetarian and was looking after myself better. I wasn't a heavy smoker, but associated it with smoking cannabis which I really enjoyed. After a while I decided I didn't want to do something so injurious to myself. I switched to taking cannabis in ways that don't involve tobacco – like eating it. Sometimes, socially, I'd go back to smoking joints, and then I would start smoking cigarettes again. It took quite a few attempts before I got free of it. For quite a long time I had occasional cravings, but now I can't stand smoky atmospheres and I don't want to smoke.

The myths that stop you stopping

A few of the compelling reasons for continuing to smoke are myths, or are based on misunderstandings or inaccurate information. These are the main ones.

I need willpower, and I don't have enough of it

CALLER I haven't got any willpower.
QUITLINE You picked up the phone and called us. That's a major step. It takes willpower to do that.

No one has a fixed amount of willpower, either too little or enough. Willpower is the psychological and emotional equivalent of muscle. However weak it is, or however little you have, you build it up by exercising it. Also, willpower alone is never enough. If your motivation for giving up smoking is based on wholly negative reasons, it is like rolling a huge boulder uphill. However strong your willpower, at a certain point you will flag and the boulder will roll downhill again – you'll be back to smoking.

QUITLINE counsellors work on motivation rather than willpower. Motivation means finding something to look forward to, a positive reason for reaching your goal. When you are motivated you don't need strong willpower. You'll be rolling the boulder downhill. As discussed before, it's the difference between 'want' and 'should'. 'Want' is motivation. 'Should' is willpower. When you are very motivated for the best reasons you will be able to exercise the willpower muscle.

If I give up smoking I'll get fat

It's true that many people put on some weight when they stop smoking, but it is a relatively small amount. Anyone who puts on a large amount of weight does so because they start eating high-calorie foods instead of smoking.

The average weight gain is around 4kg (9lbs), even less in people who have watched what they eat and increased their exercise when they've given up smoking. However, 4 percent of quitters gain over 5kg (11lbs).

I tried and failed a number of times, so didn't think I could possibly give up smoking, but I was concerned about my general health. I went on a diet that was based around healthy eating, and which also led to weight loss. I also started a daily exercise programme. Within a month I had lost half a stone, and was feeling really good about myself. That's when I began to think it was barmy to do this bad thing for my health at the same time. I was beginning to see myself as a healthy person – but how could I be if I still smoked? Suddenly I saw giving up smoking as a positive thing I could do for myself, rather than a deprivation, and one day I finished my packet and didn't buy another one. My weight-loss slowed when I stopped smoking, but I still lost another pound during the course of the next month. Previously I'd always put on weight, and thought it was inevitable. But continuing to eat the right foods and take plenty of exercise proved it wasn't.

There are a number of theories to explain why you might put on weight. It is believed that smoking increases the body's metabolic rate, which means calories are burned more quickly. This may be because the heart is stimulated to beat faster. Also nicotine may act as an appetite suppressant, so that you feel hungrier when you are not smoking. It may affect the process by which the body produces heat, which also uses up calories. It is thought that smoking lowers the body-weight set point, which is the weight to which you naturally return, whether you are trying to lose or put on weight. Stopping smoking raises the body-weight set point to a healthier level. Another theory is that an enzyme that breaks down body fat is artificially stimulated by nicotine, which means you may lose a few pounds when you start to smoke. The body then adjusts by making the enzyme less active. When you quit, it takes a few weeks for that enzyme's activity to return to normal.

But smoking affects weight distribution as well. It causes the endocrine system to store your normal body fat in an abnormal way. Studies have shown that the more you smoke, the more likely you are to put on weight round your middle. As well as being unattractive, fat stored around the waist and upper torso is associated with a higher risk of diabetes, heart disease, high blood pressure, gall bladder problems and cancer of the womb and breast.

> I'd smoked for 10 years. For the first two years I was on 40 a day, but in the two years before giving up it had gone up to 60 a day. If I hadn't reached 60 I probably wouldn't have given up. It scared me to think I'd go to 80 or 100. I gave myself three months to prepare myself psychologically, planning to give up on my birthday. The night before, I smoked everything I had and when I woke up the following day I'd given up. That was 13 years ago, and I've never had another one. It wasn't hard. Within two weeks I felt fine. I took myself off on a two month trip around Africa. I enjoyed myself enormously. I had to replace my whole wardrobe because I became really fat, but after a while the weight fell off again. I'm now back to virtually the weight I was when I was a smoker.

Smoking helps me to cope with stress

Most smokers believe that smoking helps them to cope with stress, but the truth is quite the reverse. Studies have shown that smokers are more stressed than non-smokers, and that their stress levels are directly linked to their smoking habit. Research on young smokers shows that they grow increasingly stressed as smoking becomes a habit for them.

One survey concluded that 80 percent of smokers believe that smoking relaxes them. There is general agreement that stress and irritability build up when they go without for any length of time. This occurs because you are effectively withdrawing from the effects of nicotine during these periods, which makes you more tense and irritable than normal. Smoking then alleviates these feelings. Smokers are more stressed than non-smokers because the period between each cigarette is a mini withdrawal that causes stress. What you might regard as 'relaxation' is actually returning to what would be a normal mood for a non-smoker. Nicotine dependency seems to be a direct cause of stress, making smokers generally more anxious than non-smokers who have exactly the same life style or problems.

One theory suggests that smokers are more stressed because when they have a problem they may reach for a cigarette rather than dealing with it. They feel momentarily better, but the problem causing the stress remains.

Further studies have found that ex-smokers were found to be less stressed than smokers. Some other studies have found no difference between them, but no studies have found that people who had quit for good were *more* stressed than smokers.

The myth continues to be believed because the process of giving up may be stressful in itself, so for a while the quitter feels more stressed. This settles down – very quickly for some, longer for others – and the ex-smoker's mood improves when this phase is over. On average it takes two weeks for the quitter to start to feel 'normal', and, after this, anxiety levels decrease even further, and feelings of relaxation improve even more. One survey followed quitters for six months. All of those who had not gone back to smoking rated themselves as significantly less stressed than when they were smoking. Quitters who relapse, or who simply smoke less, show no obvious improvement in their stress levels.

CALLER I've smoked for 60 years. My doctor keeps telling me to give up. I had a heart attack two years ago and he says if I keep on like this it's likely to happen again. I'm ready to try, but I don't know whether I should use nicotine patches, or which ones to choose. (*They talked about the amount and strength of the cigarettes she smoked, and which products would help.*)

CALLER But will they help me with stress? I don't know how I'll cope without cigarettes. I've got all this worry about my grand-daughter, and I have trouble with the neighbours. Cigarettes help me keep calm.

QUITLINE Smoking only appears to help with stress. It's been shown that smokers are actually more stressed than non-smokers.

CALLER That's what you say. But it makes me feel stressed even thinking of coping without them.

QUITLINE You might feel stressed for a short while as you make the change, but eventually your stress levels will drop.

CALLER That's easy to say. But I know myself, and if the woman next door starts on as she sometimes does, I'll have to have a cigarette, patches or not.

QUITLINE Shall we talk about those feelings for a while, and think of other ways you might deal with it rather than smoking? (*They went on to discuss strategies that she could use at stressful times.*)

Tough stuff – the bad news about smoking

You'll have read or heard many of the ways that smoking is bad for you. It's up to you whether you decide to read it again here. Some people need to be frightened into quitting, while it makes others want to smoke more. You may prefer to read this section once you have already begun the process of giving up, rather than before you start.

Heart and circulation

Tobacco smoking accounts for 20 percent of all deaths from heart disease. Giving up smoking after a heart attack can halve the chance of it happening again. Carbon monoxide and nicotine are two chemicals in tobacco smoke that affect the heart. Carbon monoxide reduces the blood's ability to carry oxygen to the heart and all other parts of the body. In some smokers, a considerable proportion of their red blood cells are carrying carbon monoxide gas instead of oxygen round their bodies.

Nicotine stimulates the body to produce the stress hormone adrenalin, which makes the heart beat faster and so raises blood pressure and can give you a jittery feeling.

Strokes

Strokes are a bigger killer than cancer, and 18 in every 100 deaths from strokes are associated with smoking. Chemicals in cigarette smoke fur up the arteries which carry oxygen around the body. A stroke occurs when a portion of the brain is deprived of oxygen due to clogged arteries. This damages the brain to the point where you can die, or never fully recover from the effects – for instance you may lose the power of speech.

Peripheral vascular disease (PVD)

Smoking can cause blocked blood vessels in the legs or feet. This can cut off the supply of oxygen to the legs, which results in gangrene. The cure is amputation. Smokers have a 16 percent greater risk of developing PVD than people who have never smoked. The majority of cases of PVD which lead to amputation are caused by smoking.

Cancer

After heart disease and stroke, cancer is the biggest killer in the Western world. It's estimated that 90 percent of cases of lung cancer are caused by smoking. Smoking is also a factor in one-third of all other cancers, due to the wide range of harmful chemicals it introduces into the body (4000 in each cigarette). The other main cancers with links to smoking are: mouth, lip, throat, larynx, bladder, kidneys, cervix, pancreas, oesophagus, stomach and duodenum.

Smoking causes damage over a long period. Lung cancer can take 20 to 30 years or more to develop. Smokers who inhale draw a mass of harmful chemicals and gases into their lungs. Then a dark, treacly tar is deposited and gradually absorbed. The cancers caused by smoking tend to develop in the part constantly exposed to the chemicals, mainly the lungs.

Respiratory disease

Apart from lung cancer, smoking adversely affects your breathing and respiratory health in other ways.

Chronic obstructive lung disease

Chronic obstructive lung disease, which includes chronic bronchitis and emphysema, is progressively disabling. It causes obstruction or narrowing of the airways in the lung and the destruction of the air sacs. This makes breathing difficult and painful. The lung becomes less elastic and less able to absorb oxygen.

This is a disease that creeps up on you. Once you have noticed the breathlessness, about half your lung has been destroyed. At its most severe, sufferers need to carry an oxygen cylinder around with them.

It is very rare for non-smokers to suffer from this disease, which is not reversible.

Pneumonia

Pneumonia is much more common among smokers than non-smokers, and smokers are more likely to die from the disease.

Sex and fertility

Becoming pregnant

Women who smoke may be less fertile than non-smokers. Smokers usually take longer to conceive than non-smokers. The menopause also tends to occur two years earlier in smokers, so reducing the time a woman is able to become pregnant. Women smoking more than ten cigarettes a day have an increased risk of an early menopause. It has been estimated that women who smoke are only three-quarters as fertile as others. The sperm of male smokers has also been found to be less healthy.

Impotence

Because smoking affects the circulation, male smokers have more trouble getting or maintaining an erection, which depends on a healthy blood supply to the penis. This blood supply can be reduced by up to a third. One study of men between the ages of 31 and 49 showed a 50 percent increase in the risk of impotence among smokers compared with men who had never smoked. A study of men suffering from potency problems who attended a sex clinic found that a significant proportion were smokers or ex-smokers. Smoking increases the risk of impotence by around 50 percent for men in their thirties and forties.

Smoking and pregnancy

Each cigarette you smoke affects your unborn baby's development. Oxygen supply to the baby is reduced, which makes the baby's heart beat faster and means the baby grows more slowly. Fewer nutrients get to your baby through the umbilical cord.

You are likely to have more complications during your pregnancy if you smoke. Smokers are more likely to have a miscarriage, to bleed during pregnancy, for their waters to break early (putting the baby at risk of infection), or giving birth prematurely.

Babies born to smokers are on average 200 grams lighter than others. Smaller babies are much more likely to pick up infections and other diseases once they are born, including meningitis. There is evidence to suggest that this has a continuing effect on the child's physical growth and intellectual development. The earlier you give up the more likely it is that your baby will be a normal weight and avoid the long-term problems.

The risk of your baby being born dead, or dying within one week of birth, is increased by about one third if you smoke. Later on, more than one-quarter of the risk of death due to Sudden Infant Death Syndrome (SIDS; cot death) is connected to parents smoking.

Breast feeding

Smoking cigarettes can affect the milk you produce, both in quantity and quality. Nursing mothers pass nicotine to their baby. The children of smokers are much more likely to suffer from illnesses of the ears, nose, throat and lungs due to passive smoking. Children who grow up in homes where one or both parents smoke are twice as likely to smoke themselves.

Your looks

Smoking has an effect on the way you look. As mentioned earlier, it may artificially keep down your weight, but it is likely to cause you to store fat around your middle, in an unattractive and unhealthy way. It also has a bad effect on your skin, and causes you to look older than your age.

Smoking and your skin

Smokers in their forties often have as many facial wrinkles as people in their sixties. This is because smoking dries the skin, and blood flow to the skin's surface is reduced, meaning that it doesn't get enough oxygen and essential nutrients to stay smooth and healthy looking. Research suggests that smoking reduces vitamin A in the body, which is vital for protecting against damage from the sun. Smokers also have less elastin in the skin, the protein that keeps it supple. The actions involved in smoking: squinting against the smoke and the puckering of the mouth involved in taking a puff, also encourages the development of premature wrinkling. Drawing hard on each cigarette can lead to a permanently gaunt, hollow-cheeked look.

Smokers's skin tends to look greyish, and loses its bloom. Fingers, fingernails, and teeth (especially) can become yellowed and dingy-looking.

Psoriasis

Smokers are two to three times more likely to develop psoriasis, a chronic skin condition that leads to disfiguring patches of red, dry and flaky skin, which can be itchy and uncomfortable. Smoking is implicated in about one quarter of all cases of psoriasis.

Are you ready to quit?

CALLER (crying) You've got to help me give up smoking.

QUITLINE You sound distressed.

CALLER Yes, I am. My mother died recently, and they're laying people off at work. My husband says he's got his own troubles and I should just pull myself together. We're yelling at each other all the time. If only I could give up smoking!

QUITLINE You feel it's one thing you could have control over?

CALLER Well there's certainly nothing else at the moment.

(*They explore this further for a few minutes*)

QUITLINE It sounds as if you have more than enough to cope with now.

CALLER I don't feel I can take any more!

QUITLINE It can be difficult to quit smoking when you're emotionally vulnerable and under a lot of stress. It might be better to wait until things are more settled.

CALLER I thought you'd tell me I had to stop at once! I'm worried there will always be something that stops me.

QUITLINE You sound as if you're getting to the point where you really want to stop.

CALLER I do feel more serious about stopping than ever before. But I'm frightened about whether I'll be able to cope without smoking.

QUITLINE Maybe now would be difficult, but in a couple of months it could be easier. Right now you need to take the pressure off yourself. Pressure comes when you set yourself up for something at which you're likely to fail. It sounds as if this is a really awful time for you.

CALLER It is a relief that you haven't given me a big lecture. I actually feel less like smoking because you haven't said I can't!

QUITLINE Continue to call us, and when you're feeling better and readier we can help you in your resolve to stop.

When you are going through an exceptionally difficult period, giving up smoking might be more than you can handle. While the 'ideal' time may never arrive, some moments in your life are less conducive than others to taking on this life changing project. It helps to have some emotional time and space to give to it for the best chance of success. On the other hand, if you don't really want to stop you'll always be able to find an excuse for why now is not the time. Continue to think about it; continue to work on your reasons for stopping, and why doing so will improve the quality of your life. The moment will come when you are ready, and can begin the preparations for stopping. The next chapter will help you get there.

Chapter Two

Preparing to stop

You know you are ready to quit smoking when you start to contemplate *when* you are going to do it, rather than simply thinking about it in general terms. It could be an instantaneous decision. The moment is right: you are full of resolve, or can't bear the thought of smoking any more, so you just stop. This can, of course, work:

> I'd had a really heavy night out. I can't remember how much I drank, but I certainly recall going to the cigarette machine twice in the evening, and I already had a full packet with me when I arrived. I've never felt so ill in my life as I did the next day. The first thing I saw when I woke was the ashtray over-turned on the carpet by my bed. One cigarette was only just started, but fortunately the ashtray had fallen on top of it, so it had gone out without burning anything. I realised I'd been so pissed that it could have set the place alight and I was so dead to the world

that I might have died in reality. I felt so hugely disgusted with myself, and so desperately ill, that I decided then and there never to smoke or drink again. That was five years ago. I haven't completely stopped drinking, but I've never had another cigarette. One good thing is that even on the occasions I do drink too much I don't suffer from hangovers in the same way. There's something about the way nicotine interacts with alcohol that makes for a really bad hangover.

Many people find, however, that the burst of enthusiasm or disgust that leads them to give up on impulse isn't sustainable. Once it wears off, they find themselves drawn to smoking again – either because the craving becomes too strong, or because they are in a situation where smoking seems attractive, or because they are faced with the kind of emotions they've always handled in the past by smoking.

QUITLINE counsellors have discovered that the people with the best chance of succeeding have planned to give up with some care. They've chosen an appropriate date, with reference to what will be going on at that time to make it easier on themselves. They've also looked ahead to what will be most difficult for them when they are not smoking, and planned how they are going to deal with situations and events that are likely to make them more vulnerable to a relapse.

CALLER It says in my magazine that smoking ages your skin. I know it sounds vain, but it's the first thing I've read that makes me want to give up. I'm twenty-six and I smoke 20 to 25 a day. I know I should be worried about what it's doing to my health, but I'm much more worried about looking old. It says you get these lines round your mouth. Is it true?

QUITLINE Yes, it can be. Look at (*names a famous person*). She smokes a lot, and is much more lined than other women of her age.

CALLER (*embarrassed*) Do you think it's a very shallow reason?

QUITLINE Not at all. I'm the same age as you, and I'm also concerned about looking as good as I can for as long as possible.

CALLER That's it. I'm going to stop. I'll stop tomorrow.

QUITLINE It's great you're ready to stop. Let's look at whether tomorrow is the best time for you. You're all fired up now, but it might be better not to rush, and to think it through.

CALLER I've got the day off work, and I'll find it much easier to stop when I'm not around other people who are smoking.

QUITLINE You could stop tomorrow, or use it to plan how you are going to cope. For instance, do you want to use any help, such as nicotine patches?

CALLER No, if I'm going to do it, I want to do it without an aid.

QUITLINE Let's think through what tomorrow will be like. Will you have any cigarettes in the house?

CALLER I don't know . . . Perhaps I'll smoke them all today. Or chuck any I have left in the bin before I go to bed.

QUITLINE What's happening over the next few days? Can you foresee any difficult times?

CALLER I'm seeing my new boyfriend on Thursday. That's

going to be hard. He smokes. I really like him, and I don't know how he feels about me yet. I'm going to be nervous. (*They went on to talk about how she could cope with these nerves, and whether she'd need longer to prepare.*)

Setting a date

Choosing a date to give up is the first positive step that many people take. It could be New Year's Day, following on from a New Year's Eve resolution, or 'No Smoking Day'. Both of these dates, apart from being symbolic, are popular because you know that many hundreds or thousands of smokers are quitting alongside you, even if you don't know them personally.

Other people choose a date with more personal significance, such as a birthday, the end of exams or a big project, or the start of a holiday.

My father rang me the week before my birthday. Smoking was beginning to get to me. My chest was feeling tight, and I told him. He said, 'Why don't you stop?' For some reason, something clicked. I said, 'OK I will.' And I did on my birthday. I'd gone through periods of giving up before, for about six months at a time, but I always went back. This time I never did.

But there doesn't have to be a special reason to stop. It's more important to pick a time when you will be least susceptible to temptation, and when circumstances support your resolve to give up – when you can avoid the situations that usually make you want to smoke. It should be a period of relative calm. You can never ensure that stressful situations won't arise, but you can plan for the most likely time. There are always exceptions to any rule, however, and like this quitter, you might actually find that a difficult time is paradoxically a good moment to give up:

> I gave up when I was going through hell. I'd just broken up with my boyfriend after he insisted I had an abortion, and I was grieving for him and for my lost baby. My freelance work was drying up and I didn't know how I was going to make money. I worried that I'd lose my flat, and I'd have to move back with my parents. I thought: I can't feel worse than this, so one more bit of suffering isn't going to make much difference. Actually, focusing on giving up and staying stopped helped me take my mind off the worse things that were happening. Also, because I was saving the money that usually went up in smoke I felt I was at least making a positive contribution to my dire finances.

Usually, though, QUITLINE counsellors find it helps to choose a less stressful time. If you are very distressed, or are particularly challenged because of moving house, changing jobs, going through a divorce, or anything else that depletes your energy and your resources, giving your attention to quitting might be more than you can manage. A relapse is more likely in these circumstances, and going back to smoking may feel like a failure that adds to the pressures you are already under.

The point of planning is to work out when would be a good time. As well as stressful occasions, try to avoid giving up just before major celebrations, such as parties or weddings. These can be triggers for some smokers, for a number of reasons. If it's an important occasion for you, there may also be additional stress. If smoking is associated with increasing your enjoyment and pleasure, you could be carried along by the joy of the moment and want to light up. You are also likely to drink more alcohol on these occasions, and for many smokers the two go together – or alcohol makes you forget why you were so resolved to stop in the first place.

ACTION Get your calendar or diary and work out when in the near future is the most appropriate date to stop, and when you will be most likely to be able to stay stopped. Think through the implications. Would a weekend be easier because you won't be affected by the stress of work or workmates who smoke? Or conversely would a weekday be easier because smoking is not allowed at work so your first few hours of going smoke-free would be supported? Would evening or daytime be better?

Before the date arrives, become a more conscious smoker. If you haven't done so already, think about each cigarette you smoke, and write down your feelings about it (see page 13). Before giving up it helps some people to regard smoking as a duty, in order to observe your reactions to it. Sometimes, feeling that you must do something makes you want to do the opposite.

Cutting down or giving up completely?

Some people experiment with their readiness to give up by cutting down first. Many of these aim to cut down so far that the step to giving up finally is easier to take.

Cutting down certainly helps you to find out more about what makes you smoke – and pinpoints what might be the hardest thing for you in giving up. It is an excellent learning process, but it rarely makes it easier to quit for good.

This is because the fewer you smoke, the more time you spend thinking about smoking. The constant question in your mind is likely to be: 'When can I have the next one?'

People who cut right down also often find that the ones they do smoke become even more pleasurable, because they are the 'essential' cigarettes that give them most satisfaction, such as the first one of the day. Research has shown that most people need approximately seven cigarettes a day to stop them going into withdrawal, depending on how they are spaced out. When you get below seven it is almost as easy to cut out all cigarettes completely; some people find it easier.

It is also common to smoke those last remaining cigarettes more heavily, inhaling more deeply, and smoking them right down to the bitter end. The other problem is that if you continue to smoke a few, the temptation to increase your consumption is less avoidable when you are stressed or enjoying yourself.

CALLER I used to smoke a packet a day and I've now cut

down to two or three cigarettes at most. But my husband still goes on at me to stop.

QUITLINE Why's that?

CALLER I'm at home with the kids, and he says it's no good for them. He's right, but he's one to talk – he's smoking as much as ever. I know he's not around them when he smokes, but he doesn't have to put up with what I do.

QUITLINE You're down to just a couple?

CALLER Yes. Well, usually. Sometimes I have such a pig of a day that I have smoked more than that. I had a bad week last week, but I'm sure I can get it down again.

QUITLINE You've done really well cutting down so much. Did you know it's even harder to cut down than to give up completely? You keep experiencing withdrawal symptoms while you're still smoking, but when you give up properly they eventually go away. Do you want to discuss how you can do this?

Planning your quitting strategy

Stopping is one thing. Becoming an ex-smoker and quitting forever is another. What helps you move towards this goal is having strategies to support you at the various danger points, when you are at risk of relapsing. The main ones are: coping with physical withdrawal, breaking the habit, and coping with the situations or emotional pressures that have always been accompanied or managed by smoking.

Physical withdrawal varies from person to person. For some people it is not a problem, or much milder than they envisaged.

You're unlikely to know whether it will be hard or easy for you until you have actually stopped. Physical withdrawal is looked at in detail in Chapter 4. Breaking the habit and coping with trigger situations can be planned in advance. We'll look at these in the rest of this chapter.

The power of habit

It has been said that nicotine is as addictive as heroin and, therefore, that every quitter must anticipate a period of painful withdrawal. Some smokers call QUITLINE obviously very worried about this: if the chemicals are more addictive than heroin, will it mean suffering worse than a heroin addict while breaking the dependency? Few people relish pain, and will do anything to stop it in the short term. Thinking about the short-term pain involved in stopping smoking can put you off attempting it, because the long-term pain associated with smoking-related diseases, such as cancer or emphysema, seems too far off to worry about now.

In fact, although nicotine is extremely addictive, a substantial proportion of quitters don't suffer much physically when their supply is taken away from them. Much of the difficulty that many smokers experience when giving up is more to do with breaking the habit. What many people call 'craving' and believe is a desire for nicotine, is really missing the mechanical actions of smoking – opening the packet, or making roll-ups; lighting up; the action of taking puffs and blowing out the smoke; tapping the cigarette on the ashtray; having something to do with your hands and mouth at regular intervals.

If you've ever tried to break any habit, you'll know it's difficult. Whether it's biting your nails, interrupting someone instead of listening, stopping saying 'you know' or another verbal mannerism, slouching instead of sitting straight, talking with your mouth full. Try falling off a bicycle, when you've developed the habit of riding one properly. It's not easy.

Through the early days of giving up it can help to consider that you may be missing the habit rather than craving nicotine. If you believe it's a drug-related craving you'll feel more helpless. If you believe the difficulty is only connected to missing nicotine you'll wonder why you still find it hard even if you are using nicotine replacement therapy (NRT), which is continuing to supply you with the nicotine. On the other hand, knowing that much of your discomfort is because of the process of becoming used to living without a habit can make it more manageable. One QUITLINE counsellor often suggests the following experiment to callers:

ACTION Before the day you've chosen to give up smoking, experiment by breaking another habit. If you find it difficult to think of a habit of yours, ask friends if they've noticed a habit you might not be aware of. It could be something like playing with your hair, nodding, tapping your foot, or a word or phrase you use often. Spend a couple of days being aware of this habit, and attempting to stop it. This might be more difficult than you think. When you do give up smoking, however, you'll be better able to separate the feelings associated with the loss of the habit from the nicotine cravings, and know that you'll be able to manage them.

Strategies to help as you break the habit

When you have stopped and before you have broken the habit, smoking will be on your mind throughout the day. Every so often you will forget that you've stopped, and want to reach for your cigarettes. This is also true, of course, if you are suffering from withdrawal symptoms and are craving nicotine. The occasions when you will miss your habit are different for everyone. Look back at the lists you made in your notebook: the reasons you find smoking pleasurable or necessary, and when you smoke and why. You may have identified the habitual moments already. Perhaps you always light up when your favourite soap starts on television, or you like to settle in with a cigarette the minute the telephone rings and you know it's a friend or family member to whom you'll chat for some time. Perhaps smoking acts as punctuation marks in your day – five minutes during which you step outside for a cigarette. Now is the time to plan what you will do at those moments, when you are feeling vulnerable and the desire to smoke becomes strong. You can expect to feel twitchy for a few days at least.

I started smoking at the age of fourteen and carried on for 28 years, smoking about 30 a day. I've never seriously tried to quit in the past and couldn't believe that it wasn't difficult. I used the nicotine gum for the first few days, and that certainly stopped the craving for nicotine. It was the actual habit of smoking – what to do with your hands syndrome – that bothered me, but that passed after about two weeks. When we used to go out my partner would say, 'Don't forget your ciggies', which was a message to me to put a packet of gum in my handbag.

Fortunately, the acute craving or the disorienting feeling when you automatically want to reach for a cigarette before you remember that you've quit, usually lasts only a few minutes at most. The best prepared people work out in advance a list of five-minute activities they can refer to at those moments, and pick the one they most fancy. The following tip is a way that you can make a game of this, and it has been successfully used by many quitters:

ACTION Write a list of things you can do that last for about five minutes. Cut it up, so that each activity is on a separate piece of paper. Put them in a bowl that you will keep handy when you stop smoking. When you feel a craving, or a habitual desire to reach for a cigarette, reach for one of the pieces of paper instead. Either close your eyes and choose at random, or read through and choose the most appropriate tip according to your mood. It can help if it involves some sort of movement. Simply going from one room to another to do something can shift your attention from the craving. Things that involve your mind and your hands are especially useful.

50 ways to beat your habit

Here are 50 ways that have helped people who phoned the

QUITLINE. Some of them last longer than five minutes, some of them won't appeal, but all will take your mind off smoking for a while. Use this list to prompt you to come up with ideas of your own.

1. Chop up some vegetables or fruit into bite-sized pieces, which you can put in the fridge for when you are feeling peckish. This will also stop you reaching for more high-calorie snacks if your appetite increases.
2. Clean your teeth
3. Wash your hands.
4. Juice some fresh fruit or vegetables.
5. Make a cup of tea or coffee, or pour yourself some water or juice.
6. Take yourself off for a walk round the block.
7. Phone a friend.
8. Phone QUITLINE (0800 002200) – there is no limit to how many times in a day you can do so.
9. Clean out a drawer.
10. Do the washing up.
11. Place some more pieces in a jigsaw.
12. Water your plants.
13. Go into the garden and do some dead-heading, weeding, digging or other chore.
14. Get on with some decorating.
15. Breathing exercise No. 1: Lie down or sit comfortably with one hand placed on your abdomen and the other on your chest. Push on your abdominal muscles when you breathe in, then pause, and feel the muscles pushing

against your hand as you breathe out. There should only be a little movement in your chest. This will help you become aware of breathing slowly and deeply. Aim to breathe 12 to 15 times a minute.

16. Breathing exercise No. 2: 'SOS' – Sigh Out Slowly. Breathe in deeply, then release your breath very slowly and gently as a sigh, until your lungs are empty. Or you can count out aloud under your breath as you do so – you'll notice how much higher you can count as the days without smoking go by, and your lungs clear.

17. Clean a window.

18. Clean a pair of shoes.

19. Sort out some paperwork

20. Take the dog for a walk.

21. Do a couple of clues in a crossword puzzle.

22. Read a few pages of a book or newspaper.

23. Play a computer game for a few minutes.

24. Do a few more rows of your knitting, sew on a button, take up a hem, or do some more work on a garment you're making. Or work further on a piece of embroidery.

25. Practice your juggling skills. Keep a how-to-juggle book and some soft balls handy.

26. Take out your 'why I want to give up smoking' list and read it. Add any new thoughts that occur to you.

27. Make an entry about your craving in your notebook. Put down the time, what you are doing, and why you think you particularly desire to smoke at this moment.

28. Take out the jar where you are putting the money you would otherwise spend on smoking and count it.

29. Play a hand of patience or build a house of cards.

30. Count down backwards from 100.

31. Write a postcard to a friend.

32. Write an e-mail to a friend, reporting how many hours or days you've spent not smoking.

33. Stand on your head.

34. Ask a colleague if there's anything you can help with.

35. Clip or file your nails, or paint them with varnish.

36. Add up how many seconds it is since you last smoked.

37. Practise a magic trick.

38. Practise an instrument.

39. Sing.

40. Walk or run up and down the stairs three times.

41. Sort the clothes in your wardrobe into colour-co-ordinated sets.

42. Fill a bag with unwanted items for donating to a charity shop.

43. Arrange your books, videos or CDs into alphabetical order.

44. Work out how many cigarettes you smoked last year, and what it cost you.

45. Stroke an animal.

46. Ask someone for a cuddle.

47. Put on your favourite music and dance.

48. Tidy up some mess in another room.

49. Make a start on preparing your evening meal.

50.   Do some colouring-in – in a child's book, or black-and-white pictures in the newspaper.

Strategies to help deal with situations in which you are tempted to smoke

> When I gave up smoking I found it helpful to avoid the situations in which I used to smoke. I (temporarily) avoided pubs and social gatherings with smoking friends. I had a mental list of activities to embark on at those times when I would have smoked; for example, when having a coffee, I'd sharpen all the kids' colouring pencils, or I'd manicure my nails – anything that kept my hands busy. Most helpful of all, I started dating a non-smoker! I haven't smoked now for about seven years.

Every smoker knows that there are places and situations that are inextricably associated with smoking. These are when you automatically smoke, whether you really want to or not, and where you tend to smoke even more than usual. Because these tend to be public places, you are unlikely to be able to use your list of habit-breaking displacement activities, and are reduced to relying on willpower alone.

For many people it helps to plan to avoid these as much as possible in the early days of giving up smoking when you are most likely to relapse. You don't have to avoid them forever, just until you are more secure as an ex-smoker. As you conquer the cravings and the habit you will be better able to manage being in these situations without smoking.

Typically, these are pubs and clubs, where you drink

alcohol, and where smokers congregate. Change your routine for a while, and if necessary explain to your friends why you are keeping away. Other tempting situations include: spending an evening with a friend with whom you've always particularly enjoyed smoking, and who does not want to give up; slipping out of work for a few minutes with the smoking gang; at a meal in a restaurant where everyone lights up at the end.

ACTION Look back at the lists you made earlier, or make a new one now. List situations like these when you know you will be powerfully tempted to smoke. Imagine the situation. Imagine how you will feel. If you have given up before, and been tripped up into starting again by one of these situations, remember what happened and why you gave in. Plan what you are going to do. Avoid them for a while? Or is there something else you can do to help you manage them in a different way?

It was hard at first because all my family smoke, and I was captain of a darts team, who all smoked. I bought a pack of nicotine chewing gum and had that if the urge to smoke got to me. I carried round two packs of cigarettes so that I knew I could have one if I got really desperate, but I never had to have one.

Strategies to help deal with emotions

For most smokers smoking is more than a physical addiction.

Smoking is a prop, a friend, a reward. Even more importantly, you often smoke at key emotional moments, either to enhance your feelings (of pleasure; of seeming cool or hard) or because you are uncomfortable with your feelings and want to change them. Smoking is a way you can avoid distress or take your mind off it for a short while. Planning to prevent a relapse, therefore, means understanding which emotions you have become accustomed to handling or avoiding by smoking, and thinking creatively of other ways you can manage them.

ACTION Look back at the lists you made about why you smoke, or make a list now. Which emotions trigger a desperate need to smoke? If you've given up before, think of what made you go back to smoking – was there a particular emotion attached to it? Make a new list: 'I most need to smoke when . . .'

You'll probably notice that there are two broad categories of emotional triggers: those that crop up every day, and those that are connected to crises.

Daily emotional triggers aren't going to vanish – and in the early days of quitting you are likely to feel more emotional for a while, so they may even increase. Knowing what they are helps you to plan for them. Perhaps it's when the family argues or when there's a problem at work. Maybe you can't sit through a traffic jam without lighting up. Perhaps you are most vulnerable when you are hanging around with nothing to do and feel bored, or when you want cheering up.

Crises will happen from time to time, and if you associate

smoking with stress control, it may be your first recourse when something goes wrong. Again, planning alternatives in advance will help you over the hump.

It's useful to look at the most common emotions in more detail. In essence, the secret to planning for successful quitting is understanding when you use smoking as a support – and how you can get that support in other ways. Similarly, it's about understanding when you use it as a pleasure-enhancer or a reward, and deciding what you will do instead.

I most need to smoke when I'm under stress

Smoking doesn't actually help with stress – look at Chapter 1 (page 26) to remind you of the truth – but the fact is that most smokers think it does. It comes top of the list of emotions to tackle because the first couple of weeks of quitting are stressful in themselves. Making a life change (even a good one) is stressful, as is withdrawal from an addiction.

It makes sense, therefore, to anticipate that you will be under stress for a while and at some time in the future, and plan how you are going to handle it. Use what you know from other occasions when you've tried to give up. What have you done in the past to handle successfully feelings associated with stress – before you smoked, or while you were giving up? What strategies did you use?

ACTION Make a list of five to ten things you can do to help yourself, under the heading 'When I feel stressed I will . . .'

Some of the items listed in the '50 ways to beat your habit' section (see page 48) can help here. Look through them and pick the ones you'd like to try. You might want to give them a test run, now, before you give up. The two breathing exercises are particularly good. So is any form of physical exercise. As well as taking your mind off smoking, exercise has been proven to lower stress levels. It also has the benefit of making you fitter, and speeding up your metabolism so that you are less likely to put on weight. Some people decide to use the money they'll save by quitting to join a gym – and some people who have trouble with stress find karate or judo classes helpful, or other ways to help them work off aggression.

You don't have to spend any money at all to increase your exercise. Taking up jogging, a sport, or walking when you would usually catch the bus, the train, or hop in the car, are all practical alternatives. Using the stairs, instead of a lift or escalator also helps. Even something that doesn't immediately strike you as exercise, such as gardening, is physically strenuous, and therefore calming. Working amid nature, even in a non-physical way, also brings peace. If you don't have your own garden you could offer to help a friend. Something like fishing is calming, as is anything that involves work with a satisfying end-product, such as cleaning or decorating.

More obviously calming activities, such as yoga, T'ai Chi, or learning meditation are useful options. An evening class in meditation will give you tools you can use throughout the day. When you organise your life to include a number of calming or relaxing activities, it takes longer for you to reach your stress 'flash point', so even in a critical situation you feel less stressed and better able to cope.

Think ahead to how you can plan for the daily situations that are stressful. If you're irritated by driving in heavy traffic, for example, leaving half an hour earlier than usual will immediately take the pressure off. Playing gentle and soothing music in the car is better than music with too much pace or beat, which can make you tense, even if you enjoy it. Gentle music is also preferable to listening to disturbing news on the radio.

CALLER I stopped smoking at Christmas, and I was doing so well. I thought I'd never go back to it. Then I went on holiday with my new partner. I was really looking forward to it. He seemed to get on so well with my little boy before, but he irritated the hell out of him on holiday. He obviously wished I'd left him behind. I was piggy in the middle, so I started smoking again, and I haven't stopped since. I'm now back to ten a day, and I hate myself for it. I feel really ready to stop again now.

QUITLINE You did really well stopping for six months. What have you learned from that which will help you this time?

CALLER The nicotine chewing gum works for me. And I have to arrange a lot of things to keep me busy throughout the day. (*She listed everything else that worked for her, and what was difficult.*) This time I'll stop on a Sunday, because it's the best day. I've got two dodgy situations coming up this week – one's a party, so I won't stop this Sunday, I'll stop on the Sunday after. Next week I've got three social events, but one's with kids around so I won't smoke then and one's something else where I won't be tempted to smoke. (*She summarised what she'd do over the next couple of weeks to help herself.*)

QUITLINE What will you do if there's trouble between your partner and your son?

CALLER I'll kill myself if they start arguing again!

QUITLINE That really is removing yourself from the situation! How else could you cope with it? (*They talked through a number of options, until she had a plan of action.*)

I most need to smoke when I'm bored

Boredom is near the top of the reasons that impel a smoker to light up. It gives you something to do; it makes time pass. Boredom is more noticeable when you've just given up. You are likely to feel jittery; you're not doing anything with your hands, and it bothers you. Planning for ways to fill your time interestingly, amusingly or productively is sensible. Many of the suggestions in '50 ways to beat your habit' will help with this particular emotion. This is a good moment to plan to take up something that has always appealed to you, which you've never had time for before, or which you can finance from the money you are going to save.

ACTION Make a list of five to ten things you can do to help yourself, under the heading 'When I feel bored I will . . .'

Many people find that the best way of coping with boredom is to do something mentally involving, such as crosswords, computer games, or reading. Creative activities that stimulate your imagination and draw on your talents help alleviate boredom while also making you feel satisfied and stimulated.

> It helped me give up when I started a new tapestry. I didn't want it to smell of smoke. It came to represent my new life. It was an intricate thing to do with my hands, and so absorbing. I used to press it to my face and relish the clean smell of it.

I most need to smoke when I'm angry or irritable

Many smokers light up when something or someone has made them feel angry, or they find they are becoming snappy. It gives you pause, and may be the equivalent of 'counting to ten' before doing anything rash. Irritability is also connected to the withdrawal from nicotine, so a smoker denied a nicotine fix for a while becomes increasingly restless and impatient.

In the early days of giving up smoking, therefore, you are likely to be more irritable than usual, and if this is your weak point it is important to think through ways you will handle yourself when this happens.

ACTION Make a list of five to ten things you can do to help yourself, under the heading 'When I feel angry or irritable I will . . .'

Some of the actions on page 48 may help you here. The feelings are likely to pass as you take your mind off what is annoying you. Physical activities that use energy will most quickly and effectively disperse your angry feelings. There are also some other ploys which may be more specifically helpful:

- Remove yourself from the source of annoyance. If the children are driving you mad, or someone is making you angry, leave the room for a while. Wait for a few minutes to calm down. The breathing exercises can help here.
- Take out your aggression in a way that doesn't matter. Things that work include: screaming into a pillow, or into an empty mug (scream as loud as you like and only the tiniest noise will result as the mug fills with air). Pummel a cushion, a pillow or the mattress.
- Discover whatever it is that has been getting on your nerves. In the past, smoking has helped you put the lid on anger and irritability, making you feel better momentarily without resolving the underlying problem. Is there something you need to ask someone to start or stop doing? Are there other changes you need to make in your life that you have been avoiding? This is the time to recognise that tackling these issues is more productive than trying to control the feelings through smoking.

ACTION What or who is getting on your nerves? Write in your notebook what needs to change in your life for you to feel better. Which of these could you influence, by taking a decision yourself, or by explaining clearly to someone else what you need from them? Make a date to talk these

through with the person concerned, and look for the support
you need to take action on the matters only you can handle.

I most need to smoke when I'm nervous

Smoking when your nerves are on edge – such as just before
an exam, an interview, a hot date, a doctor's appointment,
a difficult conversation or phonecall – is a common way
smokers deal with temporary anxiety. Just as with the other
situations that cause you to light up, it doesn't actually make
it any better, but it works to distract you for a while, or
make the waiting time seem to pass a little bit faster. Because
smoking serves to increase stress, however, it is a false friend.
Nervous feelings are often connected to the general jitteriness
you experience when you haven't smoked for some time, so
you can expect to feel more nervous for a while shortly after
giving up smoking.

ACTION Make a list of five to ten things you can do to
help yourself, under the heading 'When I feel nervous I
will . . .'

The same kinds of things that help you when you feel
stressed will also help here, as the two emotions are very
similar. However nervousness usually occurs before an event
that is worrying you for some reason, and you are feeling
helpless during the waiting period, so some other tactics
can help:

- Find ways to feel more confident. Remind yourself of similar occasions where you've succeeded in the past.
- Get support. Ask a friend to accompany you, if it's appropriate, even if it's only to the door.
- Find a different way to take your mind off it. Have something to read, or phone a friend for a chat.
- Just do it. Smoking can be a way of postponing something you feel nervous about, but the postponement only serves to increase your nerves. Count to ten and take the plunge.
- Ask someone else to do it for you. If it's the kind of thing that can be delegated, ask a friend or a colleague to take it on, and offer to do something else you could manage easily in return.

I most need to smoke when I'm lonely

In some ways loneliness is similar to boredom. It's when you notice the clock ticking, and the absence of something to do. Many of the techniques that help you conquer boredom will also be useful if you're feeling lonely.

ACTION Make a list of five to ten things you can do to help yourself, under the heading 'When I feel lonely I will . . .'

Anything that brings you into contact with other people will help you when you're feeling lonely. This can involve inviting a friend over, or visiting someone, calling up a friend for a chat, or just getting out into an unfamiliar – or familiar – environment. Going for a walk will make you feel less isolated, even if you don't talk to anyone. Going to the shops, and having casual conversations with sales assistants or other shoppers also helps. Longer-term solutions include getting involved in your local community (such as neighbourhood watch schemes, tenants' association, political or religious groups, or voluntary work) or joining up with other people in a similar situation (such as single-parent groups) or people with the same interests as you.

I most need to smoke when I want a treat

Even people who would like to quit smoking, or feel the ill-effects of it as they puff away, still see smoking as a reward – something easy and small and instant that they can give themselves at any time, which appears to provide a small lift to the spirits.

When you are in the process of giving up, the absence of this quick fix can make you feel deprived. Given that you will have stopped smoking, you'll want to congratulate yourself, or feel you deserve a treat. If you're worried about putting on weight, it's especially important to work out in advance how you are going to reward yourself. When you make no plans, the easiest substitute is some food, and many smokers go for the equally quick (but high-calorie) fix of sweets, chocolate or crisps.

ACTION Make a list of five to ten things you can do to help yourself, under the heading 'When I feel in need of a treat I will . . .' Make sure that most of your treats do not involve food.

Look at the list of '50 ways to beat your habit' (see page 48), and pick out the ones you'd consider a treat. Usually it will be something that makes you feel good about yourself – either because it contributes to making you look good, or because it builds your self-esteem. This is where other people can help as well. Enlist a few trusted friends, and tell them that you need encouragement and praise. When you want a reward, call them up and tell them how you are progressing, so that they can congratulate you. It can also help to earmark the money you are saving for small daily treats, rather than a longer-term goal. You might wish to set aside your cigarette money, and make sure you spend it on minor luxuries or pleasures every day, such as magazines, books, CDs, computer games, soaps and other bath-stuffs.

I most need to smoke when I'm having fun

For some people, smoking is inextricably linked to enjoying themselves. When they are having a good time, lighting up makes them feel even more carefree. Enjoying themselves without smoking can seem much harder, if not impossible. If this is your weak point, then your danger moment will come when you're in a situation that makes you think: 'What the hell? Life's too short! I'm going to smoke!' Fortunately, people who feel like this eventually find that life is more enjoyable when they've given up for good.

This is particularly worth planning for, because you are likely to have these thoughts and feelings in a social situation, when few of the techniques mentioned so far will help you. You'll be impulsive, focused on the moment, and even if you've dealt perfectly well with the cravings for nicotine and broken the habit, you may be tempted.

ACTION Make a list of five to ten things you can do to help yourself, under the heading 'When I want to increase the fun I'm having I will . . .'

One of the most helpful things in this situation is to prepare yourself before an event or social occasion at which you know you're going to be having great fun. This is the time to go through your lists to remind yourself why you want to give up smoking, and to think again about the benefits of being smoke-free. It may also be helpful beforehand to enlist your friends to support you in your resolve to stay stopped: 'If I ask you for a cigarette, or go to buy some, please remind me why I want to quit. It will help me if you say . . . (tell them exactly what you'll need to hear to have the desired effect).'

I most need to smoke when I hate myself

Strange as it might appear, a minority of smokers are driven to smoke precisely because of the health risks, and because it is bad for them. Sometimes this goes so deep that you might need therapy to help you work through it. More usually, it is a feeling that comes and goes, depending on how you are feeling about yourself. If you're under-performing, not getting on with things, behaving badly to a loved one, not living up to your own standards, you might enjoy the temporary relief of smoking, while also having a sense that it is a rightful punishment. Unsurprisingly, you often experience this as depression.

> I'd given up smoking because I was pregnant, and for six months I was doing quite well. The trouble was I felt that my relationship with my baby's father was disastrous. I'd been to visit my parents, and I was about to catch the train to go back to him, when I was overwhelmed by a desperate need to break out. I bought myself a six-pack of lager and a packet of cigarettes, and I sat in the smoking compartment of the train glugging away and chain-smoking. It was glorious! I really enjoyed myself. But at the back of my mind I knew it was a death wish. I turned up on his doorstep swaying and grinning and feeling really pleased with myself. Some time later we went for counselling and our relationship turned round 100 percent. It was so good, in fact, that I trained to become a relationship counsellor myself. It was during the training that I had to work on my self-destructive feelings, and I did change them. Now I don't have the self-hate, or the death-wish, so giving up smoking the next time was a piece of cake. I have a loving relationship and, now, three fabulous children, so I have every reason to remain healthy.

ACTION Make a list of five to ten things you can do to help yourself, under the heading 'When I'm feeling self-destructive I will . . .'

The very action of making this list is important, as few people recognise the self-dislike or the destructive urge that makes them feel compelled to smoke at certain moments. When you do recognise it you are better prepared to evaluate your craving to smoke for what it is, and therefore consciously to stop yourself. What will help you most is to use tactics that help you to bolster your self-esteem. Look through the 50 suggestions (see page 48) and choose the ones that will help with this – often the ones that remind you how well you've done so far. If you feel too badly about yourself too often, then counselling or therapy might be the best help.

I most need to smoke when I want to rebel
Smoking can be an act of rebellion, particularly among young smokers. And for some adults it continues to be a form of rebellion, even if they are not conscious of it.

You might only become acutely aware of this when you give up, and find that a prolonged period of 'being good' about not smoking makes you feel dull and contrary. Then you may start smoking again quite perversely, even if you have gone past the cravings of the withdrawal period.

CALLER I've been so ill with bronchitis that I couldn't even get myself to the doctor. I couldn't walk a step without getting completely out of breath. It was really frightening. I'm much better now, but it's taken ages. I can't go through that again so this time I really am going to give up.

QUITLINE Does that mean you've tried before?

CALLER Yes, about 15 years ago. I only lasted two months.

QUITLINE Two months is good. You got yourself through the worst. Do you remember why you started again?

CALLER I don't really know. I just walked into a tobacconist

one day and bought myself a packet, and I was back on it
at once.

QUITLINE Why do you think that was?

CALLER It was my comeuppance, I think. I'd been so pious
when I quit. I told everyone how easy it was, and complained
if they lit up around me. Then I found I was fallible too.

QUITLINE You sound rather amused when you say that.

CALLER Well, I'm not a natural goody-goody! It doesn't suit
me to be conventional.

QUITLINE And does being a non-smoker seem conventional?

CALLER I suppose it does.

QUITLINE So when you think about giving up this time, how
do you feel about that?

CALLER I really want to give up, but I don't like the thought
of being dull and normal. At my great age, smoking is
probably the only rebellious thing I do.

QUITLINE So how can you stop this idea getting in your way
when you do quit?

CALLER I feel a bit childish now that I've said it. But it still
could be a problem in the future. I suppose it would bother
me less if I took up some unconventional thing, like bungee
jumping, hang gliding – anything off the wall and whacky.
That would surprise people, including me!

ACTION Make a list of five to ten things you can do to help
yourself, under the heading 'When I feel the need to rebel I
will . . .'

Look at the crazier items in the '50 ways to beat your habit' section (see page 48), and see if they give you any ideas. Examine why smoking feels like a good way to rebel: aren't you, in fact, being rather conventional? Being enslaved by an addiction takes away the choice that 'rebellion' suggests you desire.

Other strategies

Ask every ex-smoker you know what worked for them. Make a note of any strategies that appeal. There are more ideas scattered through this book, particularly in Chapter 5, Staying Stopped.

Finding people to support you

I didn't start smoking until I went to university. All my new friends there were smokers, and I wanted to fit in. I had tried it once before when I was about sixteen, but hadn't got into the habit. One evening all five us of who shared a house got rather drunk, and began to talk about stopping smoking. We decided that we weren't going to smoke ever again. It was a dare in a drunken moment: let's see who can last the longest. It became a competition – who's going to be the first to smoke? I didn't want it to be me! Two of us never smoked again. Three went back to it for a while, but quit later. What was great was having the support of everyone struggling with the same thing.

Many ex-smokers say that stopping with a friend, or their partner, made all the difference to them. It gives you someone to share the difficulties with, and the pleasure and excitement that comes with succeeding. Young people, particularly, find it helps to stop with a friend. Often young smokers are reluctant to give up because they don't want to be different from the group, so having an ally makes it possible.

YOUNG CALLER They told us about you at school. You help people stop smoking, don't you? So tell me what to do. I don't want my mum to find out I smoke.

QUITLINE What about you? We'll talk about your mum finding out later. But you're phoning now – is it because someone made you?

CALLER No, I thought of it myself.

QUITLINE Does that mean you want to stop for other reasons – for yourself?

CALLER Yes, I can't swim so far underwater any more. I keep getting out of breath.

QUITLINE How do you think you'll be happier or different if you stop smoking?

CALLER I might be chosen for the school swimming team

QUITLINE So what's stopping you from stopping?

CALLER Everyone smokes. They'll make fun of me.

QUITLINE Who's your best-friend?

CALLER Jenny.

QUITLINE Tell me about her. What makes you the best of friends? (*it transpires during the chat that Jenny also smokes and also enjoys swimming*). Have you told her that you are ringing us?

CALLER No, I don't want her to take the mick.

QUITLINE You share a lot in common – perhaps just like you Jenny could be ringing in and saying I want to stop, but not daring to tell you.

CALLER (*laughs*) I suppose so.

QUITLINE Why don't you find out what Jenny's really feeling. She may be worrying about it affecting her breathing and her swimming as well. You could give up together.

Many adults, too, benefit from having someone to quit with. It doesn't suit everyone, but if it appeals to you, start looking for a quitting partner now.

After my divorce, my son would come and stay with me in my tiny flat. He hated me smoking, and I worried about the effect of passive smoking on him. I'd given up cigarettes years before, and smoked small cigars instead. What had started as the occasional cigar after meals had crept up to being pretty near what I used to smoke in cigarettes. He was my main incentive to give up. There was also an old lady in the flat next door who had been very ill in hospital, and had been forced to give up by her doctor, and she was climbing the walls. She'd been treating me rather like a son, and I used to get her shopping in for her. We agreed to support each other in giving up. We'd pop in and out of each other's flats and drink tea together and talk about how hard it was. She'd often say wheedlingly, 'Shall we be very naughty and just have the tiniest puff?' And I'd say 'No we mustn't! Let's have another biscuit instead.' She became my second reason for giving up. I didn't want to let her down or give her an excuse to start again – her doctor had told her she'd die if she did.

ACTION Start telling other smokers your plans, and find out if any of them want to buddy up with you. Talk through how you are going to work together. It is especially helpful to know when you can call each other if you need support during a bad attack of craving: can you take private calls at work? How early and how late are you prepared to take each other's calls? Some people find it amusing to agree to a series of forfeits payable by the person who gives in and smokes first. If you live with each other, these can include: cleaning the other's shoes; making breakfast; doing an unpleasant chore. Or you might agree to a system of fines, whereby the one who relapses has to put money in a jar, for the use of the other person.

Even if you want to quit alone, it does help to have allies. Allies don't have to be other people going through the process of giving up. They might be ex-smokers, or simply non-smokers who want to help you succeed. Pick your allies with care – choose the people who will give you the kind of support you find the most helpful. Do you want a good listener who will listen to your moans? Or do you want someone who is going to cheer you on? Do you react best to a watchdog who'll keep their eye on you, or someone who will remind you regularly of the benefits of giving up? You might want a number of supporters, or find all you need in one person.

ACTION Ask one or two people if they'd be prepared to support you through giving up. Explain clearly what kind of support you would find helpful, and which unhelpful. For instance, if being nagged or lectured puts you off, say so.

Enrol your smoking friends as well. Tell them that you want to give up, and ask for their support over the more difficult early days. Ask them not to offer you cigarettes, and not to give you any if you ask.

Dealing with people who don't want you to succeed

Usually people are well-disposed towards smokers who are trying to give up, and want them to succeed. But some people don't, and will try to sabotage your efforts, or enjoy it if you fail. This tends to be more of a problem for young smokers, many of whom continue smoking because of peer pressure even when they are not fully hooked, or even when they'd really like to stop.

Many of the young people who ring QUITLINE are looking for techniques to help them parry bullying comments or behaviour from erstwhile friends. As one counsellor says, 'A sense of humour usually helps. I encourage the young person to come up with replies that will make their friends laugh. Sometimes they just need help wording a straight statement: something like, "If you want to carry on smoking, fine – do what you want, but I've had enough." If someone accuses them of being weak or babyish, I might suggest something along the lines of, "OK – if it's so easy how come *you* can't stop?" I talk them through things they might say to convince the other young people – tell them what they are going to spend their saved money on, for instance, or that it's going to make them better at sport. We role-play a bit. I ask the young person to describe the usual taunts, and we brainstorm what a good answer might be. I usually advise against the young person using excuses such as "I have a sore throat" instead of telling the truth. Better to come up with the positive reasons for quitting right away.'

YOUNG CALLER If I stop smoking the gang will pick on me and call me chicken.

QUITLINE I remember that happening when I was at school. So how long do you think they'll call you names before they get bored and pick on someone else?

CALLER Not sure. Probably about two weeks.

QUITLINE So it's not going to last forever, it'll stop after a couple of weeks, can you handle that?

CALLER I can see how it goes. They think they're so hard. That's why I started smoking, to be hard too.

QUITLINE Anyone can start to smoke. You don't have to be hard for that. It's giving up that's the real challenge. If you can give up, then you really will be hard.

Sometimes it can mean looking at whether the young person wants to remain friends with this particular gang, or find others to hang around with.

YOUNG CALLER I'm frightened no one will want to be friends with me if I stop smoking.

QUITLINE Do all your friends smoke?

CALLER My best friends do. They let me into their gang when I started smoking last year.

QUITLINE Who did you hang around with before?

CALLER Just some other girls. They're not very cool. They're not into good music (*mentions the names of a few bands*). They're rather childish, really.

QUITLINE You're not friends any more?

CALLER They want to be friends with *me*, but I prefer the new gang.

QUITLINE And the new gang make you feel bad about giving up smoking?

CALLER If you don't do things right, you're out.

QUITLINE It sounds as if your other friends treat you better.

CALLER Yes they do because I'm cooler than them.

QUITLINE How about hanging around with them instead?

CALLER I don't want to.

QUITLINE One group treat you well and don't mind if you don't smoke. The others make you feel bad. Which would you prefer?

CALLER (*doubtfully*) I don't know.

QUITLINE You don't have to make a decision now. Continue to think about it and call again. Maybe you want to try hanging out with your old friends for a while and see if you like it better than you think.

Even adults may have friends who make them feel bad about giving up smoking. Some people have tried to stop and failed, and don't want you to succeed where they didn't. Others may be people with whom you've always enjoyed smoking, who are disappointed that you are no longer going to enjoy the experience together.

> What made giving up hardest for me was the only other friend in our circle who smoked. He was so upset when I stopped, because it just left him. I know how he felt, because I used to be so relieved when he lit up, and I'd think, 'Now I can!' It made the disapproval of the others seem less important when there were two of us to share it. Nevertheless, he was wrong to do what he did. He put a lot of unfair pressure on me to start again, and was always trying to tempt me by pushing his packet in my direction at sensitive moments, such as when we'd just finished eating. I had to tell him that I was going to have to stop seeing him to make him start behaving better.

ACTION Identify who among your circle is likely to want to sabotage your attempts to give up smoking. Decide how you plan to handle this. Will you avoid these people for a while, or talk to them about your plans and ask them to support you instead of making it more difficult?

Projects that will increase your resolve

One way to increase your chances of becoming a non-smoker is to link giving up with larger goals to which you can look forward. Planning for these, at the same time as planning how you are going to handle quitting, brings pleasure to the task.

QUITLINE What are your reasons for wanting to quit?

CALLER I've got a bad chest, particularly in the morning. My husband says my breath smells like a rotting dustbin. It's also costing a lot of money.

QUITLINE What would you spend the money you saved on?

CALLER Going on holiday. With the amount I'm spending on fags, I could have the best holiday I've ever had within six months.

QUITLINE Where would you go?

CALLER I've always fancied a tropical island, but I've never been able to afford it.

QUITLINE Let's think about that for a while. Imagine yourself lying on the white sand of the beach, listening to the sea and the birds, feeling the sun on you. You haven't smoked for six months, so your chest is feeling really clear, you can breathe really easily. Your mouth is clean and fresh – tasting and smelling of mint. How do you think you'll feel?

CALLER Really peaceful. Really happy. At peace with myself. I realise that's what I want more than anything – to be at peace with myself.

Some people derive a motivating sense of enthusiasm and excitement by planning to do up their house. The money saved by not smoking easily finances the cost of materials if you decide to do it yourself, or can go towards paying a builder.

Every year hundreds of ex-smokers enter the 'Quitter of the Year' Awards, organised by QUIT. One recent finalist gradually redecorated his entire house. The activity kept him busy and took his mind off smoking. When it was complete, and looking clean and fresh, he said that it also ensured that he stayed stopped. 'I don't want to smoke any more, because I want to keep it looking as good as this. I had to paint my ceilings every year before, because the smoke would turn them yellow.' For more examples of successful Quitters of the Year, see Chapter 5.

ACTION Think of a project that you would find compelling and exciting. It could be a course; buying a computer and learning how to use it; changing jobs; getting fit; starting a family. Consider that giving up smoking is going to give you more energy, as well as more cash. How are you going to use it to feel really good?

I had smoked for nearly 30 years when I decided enough was enough. I smoked an average of 20 cigarettes as day. I had tried in the past to give up, but to no avail. I am the eldest of six children, most of whom smoked, as did my parents. My mother and two of my sisters gave up a couple of years ago. Then I decided it was time for me to give up as well. I was forty-five years old. The cost of smoking was going up, and it was just money going up in smoke. I needed a goal and I had always wanted to learn to drive. I gave up on the New Year's Eve and booked my first driving lesson two weeks later. I was hooked from the start. I had found something I enjoyed more than a cigarette. It was a nerve-wracking experience learning to drive, and many a time I could have murdered a cigarette. I failed my first driving test, but was determined to carry on. I went on to fail my second and third tests as well. I almost gave up and went back to smoking, but I resisted. I passed my fourth test seven months after my first lesson. I was so proud of what I achieved – and all because I gave up smoking. It is a great feeling to know that I have achieved two goals in the same year, and my life has never been better. I am fitter and more healthy than I have ever been in nearly thirty years. My next big aim is to get my husband to give up his pipe. But you have to want to give up. It's no good if someone forces you into something you don't want.

Saving your money

So many ex-smokers say that if only they'd saved all the money they would have spent on cigarettes they could have bought themselves something really substantial. If you don't put the money aside you won't notice it in the same way.

ACTION Open a special account now, in which you'll put the money you're not spending on cigarettes. For a while after you stop, you might want to put the money you're saving into a jar. It's satisfying to see it mount up, and to count it from time to time. Transfer it into the account when you are ready. Continue to do this until you have enough to treat yourself to something memorable. Remember to increase the amount when tobacco goes up in the budget.

Chapter Three

Stopping

On the brink of any big life change – such as going to a new school, marrying, divorcing, changing jobs, moving – it is natural to look ahead to the future and imagine what it is going to be like. It's the same with giving up smoking. For some people it's liberating to envisage themselves free from the need to smoke, feeling fitter, more carefree and more relaxed. Others find it alarming or saddening to contemplate life without smoking.

Thinking ahead in this way is not especially useful unless you find it inspiring. When you are in the process of giving up smoking the only really useful thinking you need to do is to pick your quit day, and then to concentrate on each day after that as it comes. Each day you manage to last without smoking not only contributes to your health and well-being, but it also serves to free you from the belief that a smoker is who you are, and that smoking is how you cope. Quite naturally, as the days pass, imagining yourself as a non-smoker becomes more possible and more desirable.

This chapter is about the early days of stopping, while you are becoming accustomed to this life change and to the adjustments you have to make to your habits. Quit's top ten points for successful quitting are examined in detail here.

1. Make a date and stick to it

Choose a good date for you and mark it in your diary or on a wall calender. Decide that on this day you will stop completely. You won't cut down, or have one or two to keep you going: you won't smoke at all. It is best to choose a day when this will be comparatively easy, and the temptations will be fewer than usual. This could be an exceptionally busy day, or a day when you can relax and pamper yourself; or you might prefer a day when you can arrange something really special to take your mind off smoking. It helps, also, to choose a time that is relatively unstressful, and not packed with the kinds of situations in which you most enjoy or need a cigarette.

ACTION Using your notebook as a diary from the quit day on can be interesting and helpful. Record your feelings, any cravings, the money you are saving. This can be a spur to keep going, as well as a record of your successes.

I told everybody – my wife, my children, my colleagues, the man at the corner shop where I get my supplies – that I was going to stop smoking as soon as we'd finished this major project at work that had been consuming my whole life for six months. I'd never smoked as much as I did during that incredibly stressed time. We decided to celebrate the end of the project and the start of my new healthier life. We had a party in the garden, with a bonfire and fireworks. Everyone stood around and cheered as I ceremoniously took out my Last Packet, and threw each cigarette, one by one, on the fire, and then I flung the empty packet on to it as well. I'd read somewhere that each cigarette shortens your life by five minutes, and I thought to myself: I've gained an extra 100 minutes of life, and that's just the start. I must admit that I did gulp a bit when my teenage son brought out a box of incredibly expensive cigars a client had given me, and said, 'These'll have to go as well, Dad.' But throwing them on the bonfire made me feel incredibly powerful and in control.

Preparing your home to be a non-smoking venue can mark the sense of occasion in special way. Thoroughly cleaning and deodorising carpets, curtains, bedspreads, furniture, and clothing to remove the tobacco smell can help your resolve not to pollute them again. It's also an idea to do the same with your car – thoroughly cleaning it inside, vacuuming, emptying the ashtrays and washing them clean so no smell remains. Before the day dawns, it can help to throw out any remaining cigarettes. Some people also like to get rid of ashtrays and lighters. These actions emphasise your decision.

Some people, however, like to continue to have these items

around. Indeed, some ex-smokers continue to carry cigarettes with them, long after they've given up.

> I stopped in the middle of a packet, and kept it in my bag for months, so that I knew I could smoke at any time if I really wanted to. One day someone in the pub was on the cadge, and I offered him one from the packet. His face when he lit up! They'd gone stale. It was only then that I threw them away.

Stopping on impulse

Some people prefer not to set a date, but to grab the urge to stop and act on it as and when it happens. If this works for you, then of course it is fine.

> I gave up five times, for a few months at a time, before finally stopping for good. I didn't plan for it on any of the occasions. The best way I can describe it is like a switch in my brain, flicking from smoker to non-smoker. Something would happen, and I'd think, 'That's it. I'm not smoking any more.' Although I smoked fairly heavily, I never seemed to suffer from nicotine withdrawal symptoms once the switch had flicked, and only missed the habit part for the first two or three days. I could be around smokers, I could drink, and – no pangs! I was just a non-smoker. The drawback to this was that because it was never hard, and I never had to use any willpower, it meant that when the urge came upon me to smoke some months later – either because I was having a good time, or even for no particular reason – I didn't seem to have any defences against it. I felt so in control that I was sure the odd

cigarette, or even the odd packet or two wasn't going to hurt. Of course it always did, if not immediately. But the switch had flicked to 'smoker' again and I'd be back to it before long. This time, I know I can't afford to have even a puff. And although it's been two years, I don't quite trust myself not to have a maverick moment and flick that switch once more.

Enforced quitting

Sometimes you do not plan or wish to stop, but for one reason or another you have to – your doctor warns you, or, perhaps, you have a stay in hospital where smoking is not allowed, or you feel so ill that you can't smoke, even if you want to. As already explained, being forced to stop, or stopping for reasons that don't really convince you, make it more likely that you will start again – even, sadly, if your life is in danger. But some people can use these situations to build on their own resolve.

I've spoken to many callers to the QUITLINE who've been ill, or just come out of hospital, and they've gone without smoking for a few days. They've often gone past the third day barrier – the hardest for lots of people. They're on the way, and they thought it was going to be a breeze. But then they're on the phone saying, 'My throat was terrible, and I didn't want to smoke, but I'm getting better now and the craving's setting in', or 'I was OK in hospital when I couldn't smoke, but I'm so tempted now'. They really want to stop, but they don't know how. That's when we talk about changing their routine, doing different things and keeping busy. If they haven't yet started smoking then this can work. But sometimes they've been out of hospital for a few weeks, and the smoking has crept up again, and for them it's an uphill struggle.

When you have been diagnosed with a serious illness it can be particularly distressing. If you've always coped through the bad times by smoking, it can be what you most want to do when you hear the doctor's words. If the news is very bad, you might think there is no point in giving up anyway. QUITLINE counsellors understand your conflicted feelings, and won't give you a hard time. They'll work with you to find the will and the reasons to give up smoking, if you want to.

CALLER The doc has told me I've only got three years to live if I go on smoking. He says my lungs are bad, though they feel the same as ever to me.

QUITLINE That must have been very shocking and upsetting for you.

CALLER (*shrugging it off*) Yeah, well. I gave up a few years ago for six months, so I know I can do it. Three years though . . .

QUITLINE I'm hearing you saying a very powerful thing. In your situation I would have many questions, and many thoughts about my life. I might be wondering about the point of giving up.

CALLER That's exactly how it is, love. Now that my wife's passed away, I think: what for? The fags – they're killing me, but they're my only pleasure. I don't really know what to do.

QUITLINE Cigarettes have been there for you, have been your friend – a little recipe that has worked for you in the past.

CALLER They're part of my life.

QUITLINE And how do you feel about giving up?

CALLER Last time I gave up it was when my wife, my daughter – everyone – said they couldn't stand me smoking manically one after the other. I got a book and that was quite helpful. There were a few things written in there that made me think I won't do it, and I didn't. It wasn't even hard. Now my wife's gone, my daughter's married. I lost my job, and became a cabbie. Smoking's been the only way for me to cope, and I can see myself chain-smoking forever. It doesn't make sense, does it? But what do I do when I'm waiting for a customer? I don't think much of myself for doing it. Then I think to myself: well, I am alive, and maybe it can be longer than three years, so do I really need the fags?

QUITLINE I hear you talking about lots of different feelings. You know you can give up, because you've done it, but yet you doubt it. You can't imagine not smoking, yet part of you believes you can do without it. You want to stop, yet you don't.

CALLER The main thing is, I would like to. You have to live

QUITLINE You value your life. That's a powerful reason to stop.

CALLER I looked at that book again, but it hasn't had the same effect. I've found out about lots of other ways of stopping. (*He talks about them, analysing what he's read or heard.*) I'm still trying to work out which is the best.

QUITLINE You've obviously been thinking a lot about it all. I'm hearing you telling me all these ways, and I agree with what you say. I'm just wondering whether it is most helpful for you to keep on analysing. You need to jump. How about choosing a day when it feels okay for you to stop – and then just do it?

CALLER Yeah. You're right, I can't think about it forever.

QUITLINE Pick a target date, and on that day please reward yourself. You'll be rewarding yourself anyway – you'll be investing in your future.

CALLER I like the sound of that. That's what I'll do.

QUITLINE How would you like your future to be, whether it's three years or longer? Are there things you'd like to see yourself doing, perhaps things you've never done? (*They discuss this, and the caller sounds increasingly enthusiastic and relieved.*)

CALLER I feel I can stop now. And I can use those other methods if I need to, later on.

QUITLINE I'd like to celebrate with you now that you're thinking about your future in a positive way. And on the day you take that action to stop, call us back and say I've done it – share it with us.

CALLER I'll do that, love. And I'll do it soon.

2. Keep busy

In the first few days of giving up smoking, it will come into your mind constantly. You're likely to find yourself reaching automatically for your cigarettes, as you momentarily forget that you've given up. The less you have to do, the more you will think about smoking. Planning activities, visitors or a complete change of scene will make the process much easier.

I'd heard it was tougher than coming off heroin, and I was pole-axed by the dependency I discovered I had. I decided to 'use the pain', just as Hemingway did in his writing. I started jogging, knitting, didn't go to pubs, lived from moment to moment and admitted I was addicted. I rang my dad several times a day, as he'd just given up too. I studied people who didn't smoke, so I began to build a picture in my mind of what it was going to be like. Gradually things change. The best part was finding the strength within me to face the addiction and come through. I changed, too, in interesting ways. I found I preferred fish to meat and that colours looked different to me.

ACTION If you need ideas of ways to keep busy, look back at '50 ways to beat your habit', page 48.

3. Drink lots of fluid

Drinking helps you in a number of ways. First of all, it's something to do with your hands and mouth. You can take sips from a glass that you keep by your side, just as you might reach for your cigarette and take a puff. It also helps when giving up smoking is making you hungrier, as it will quell some of the hunger pangs.

More importantly, drinking water, in particular, helps to cleanse your system. Water is good for every organ in your body. It also increases circulation, which adds oxygen to your blood, improves your bowel function and digestive system, helping to flush your kidneys, and by rapidly clearing any poisons (such as nicotine) out of your system, makes you feel better and more alert. Drinking plenty of water makes it less likely that you'll be constipated (a temporary side-effect of giving up smoking) and helps your liver work well, reducing bloating. It is recommended that you drink at least two litres of water a day (about eight large glasses) – more is even better. Water on its own is the most effective, but you can add fruit flavours, or slices of lemon or orange to give variety.

Other drinks can help to take your mind off the habit, and to quell hunger pangs, though none has quite the same cleansing effect as water. Freshly squeezed fruit juice however will also give you a healthy dose of vitamins.

It can be tempting to step up your consumption of teas and coffees, particularly if you find these drinks comforting. Watch out if you connect them too closely with smoking, though. It might be better to switch to something different, such as drinking chocolate or herbal teas if you want a hot drink, until the connection with smoking is broken. The caffeine content in tea and coffee can make you jittery if you have too much of it – also making you more likely to crave cigarettes if you've always perceived them as calming. In fact, when you stop smoking your body metabolises caffeine more slowly. This means that for the same amount of tea, coffee or cola your body will have higher caffeine levels which makes you feel even more jittery.

4. Get more active

Finding ways to put more exercise in your life will help you through the early days of giving up smoking. You will also set up habits that will make you fitter than ever for the future.

Exercise is one of the most effective ways of dealing with the build-up of emotions associated with giving up smoking – the short temper, anger or irritability, the sense of sadness or loss, and, particularly, the temporary increase in stress levels as your body adjusts to life without nicotine. When you are stressed, your body reacts as if you are in danger, by producing adrenalin, pushing up your heart rate and creating other physiological changes to help you fight or run away. When you do neither, the changes in your body are no longer good for you, and can negatively affect your health over a period of time, particularly your heart. If, instead, you use your body – in exercise or any sort of vigorous movement – your body naturally returns to a state of calm.

Physical activity helps you to relax and it also boosts your morale. Vigorous activity releases natural opiates, called endorphins, into your body. These have a feel-good effect, promoting a sense of happiness and well being. Depending on your level of fitness, ten minutes of brisk walking can be all it takes to get the endorphins flowing.

Getting more exercise into your life also means that you are less likely to put on weight when you stop smoking, and it will take your mind off any cravings. If you like the idea, you can join a gym, take up a sport, go swimming or jogging. But you don't have to do any of these traditional exercise activities to achieve a similar effect. Here are some ways to exercise more.

Ten ways to get more exercise into your life

1. Leave the car behind or don't take the bus. Walk to your destination (or at least partway) more often.
2. Take lunch hours in the park. Spend half the time walking around; feed the ducks.
3. Use the stairs instead of the lift.
4. Do some vigorous housework, such as washing the floors.
5. Dig in the garden.
6. Join in outdoor play with the children.
7. Wash the car.
8. Go dancing.
9. Rearrange the furniture in your living room.
10. Walk to pick up the takeaway, rather than having it delivered.

It is also difficult, and sometimes physically impossible, to smoke while you are doing these things, so you won't miss it as much.

5. Think positively

Very few people get through the first few days of giving up without difficulties. It's important to keep a sense of perspective, especially if you are feeling gloomy because of your decision. It's easy to become drawn into the feelings, and to believe that this is what living without cigarettes is like, when, in reality, it is a temporary phase caused by withdrawal symptoms. Keep in mind that these feelings will pass quite quickly, within a few weeks at most, and remember the benefits you are aiming towards.

CALLER I've been wanting to stop for ages and feeling so terrible about smoking. What I'm doing to my health – I'm forty-three – and what I'm doing to my two children. Last night I was so distraught about the fact that I hadn't stopped that I was crying and crying and so I made the decision at last. I've got rid of everything and I haven't smoked today. Now I'm in tears because I am stopping. I don't know what to do. I'm in tears if I don't and I'm in tears if I do. And why? Why does it hurt so much? Why is it so upsetting?

QUITLINE It can feel like a bereavement. As if your best friend has gone.

CALLER Oh yes! That's exactly what it's like! But why?! How can something like smoking have this effect on me? It's disgusting that there's this legal drug that takes you over! (*They discuss the various ways smoking creates a dependency.*)

QUITLINE Although it's very difficult for you now, and although you feel very emotional and very bad about it, you must also acknowledge what a brave step you've taken. Even though you feel terrible, you've got rid of all your cigarettes, and phoned us instead of rushing out to buy some more. That's fantastic! It's not easy for you, and you've shown real strength.

CALLER I suppose so. Thank you for saying that. I've been feeling so stupid and hopeless. But I'm also worried, because I did give up six years ago, and then I went back to it after a few months. Am I going through all this hell for nothing?

QUITLINE You've shown you can do it by stopping for a few months. You're more likely to be successful this time, because you know what is going to be difficult for you, so you can plan for it. (*They talked about why she started smoking again, and how she could avoid it this time.*) Many people tell me their self-esteem goes up when they're not smoking. They feel in control again when they're not doing something they don't want to do, so they feel better about themselves. Did you have this experience?

CALLER Yes, I did. I felt so much better about myself, which was why it was so awful that I started again. I felt better in so many ways. (*She went on to list the benefits she'd experienced through not smoking.*)

QUITLINE All that is what you are going to feel again; that is what you've got to look forward to. It might seem dark at the moment, but you're going in the right direction, as you know. Think how much better you will feel about yourself before too long – and more than that: more energetic and happier as you did before.

CALLER Thank you for reminding me. I feel I can cope with the day now.

You'll feel more positive if you have support to draw on at this time. QUITLINE (0800 002200) can help to boost your spirits for a while. Some people ring every day, and more than once a day, during the first and hardest days of quitting, so that they can hear a friendly voice and be reminded of what they are doing well. If you're feeling down, or it momentarily seems too hard, you'll be congratulated on how well you've done so far, and helped to muster your resources for the next few hours. Friends and family can be an even more constant support. Talk especially to people who have given up successfully and are now living happily without smoking.

Having a sense of humour about the difficulties also helps.

YOUNG CALLER I've been trying to give up. I did really well for two days, but I had four today.

QUITLINE Why do you want to give up?

CALLER I play football, and I've been finding the running harder.

QUITLINE Oh, who do you support? (*Caller names a team.*) And which team do you hate? (*Caller names another team.*) And what are their colours? (*Caller describes them.*) OK: those are the colours of the nicotine gremlins. Sounds as if it was four-nil to the nicotine team today. How about making it three-nil tomorrow? Remember, the gremlins are scoring every time you light up.

ACTION Look back at the lists you made about why you want to give up smoking, and how your life will be better when you are smoke-free.

6. Change your routine

When smoking has been part of your life, your daily routine and habits will serve to remind you constantly of what you are missing. That's why, in the first few vulnerable days, doing things differently can help you make the change to being a non-smoker without having to battle against these associations. In a very short while you will be able to resume your normal routine, if you want to, without it being a problem.

What needs changing temporarily is anything that triggers the automatic desire to smoke: avoiding the places where you usually smoke; not doing the usual things you associate with smoking; varying your daily pattern when it is connected to buying or smoking cigarettes; choosing to be around people who will support your desire to give up, rather than challenge it.

The pub, social club, smokers' corner or outside the front door at work are some of the more obvious places associated with smoking. Finding substitutes for these, at least for a while, will help in your efforts to break the habit. If you are homebound, and therefore everything about your usual environment makes you think about smoking, you might need to be more radical. Give up when you go on holiday, or arrange to stay with a friend, or fill your time with visits to see people, especially non-smokers, or in venues where smoking is frowned upon.

CALLER I've given up for three weeks but I went to the pub last night and had two cigarettes and I feel really bad as that's my weak point. I don't want to give up drinking as well as smoking, so I don't think I'll ever be able to stay stopped because I don't think I'll ever be able to go to a pub without smoking a cigarette.

QUITLINE So: you really enjoy going to the pub. You've avoided going for the last four weeks but you really feel you want to, and lo and behold the first day you went in you lapsed. So what's that about? What do you enjoy about the pub – the social atmosphere or the drink?

CALLER Well it's actually being with my friends. I don't want to be a social outcast. I knew the minute I'd had a few drinks that I was just going to take that cigarette and nothing mattered. I would have killed for that cigarette.

QUITLINE All right so what would it be like being in the pub without having a drink – just a fruit juice?

CALLER I couldn't imagine doing that for the rest of my life.

QUITLINE It doesn't have to be for the rest of your life – just until you've got over this point where you're quite vulnerable. It's quite a tricky one, because after a couple of drinks your willpower and control go. Or you forget why it was you decided not to smoke. So what do you want to do? You had your lapse last night and you're feeling really bad this morning. How do you want to proceed?

CALLER This is always the danger point for me. I've given up six times before, and this is the thing that gets me. I don't think I'll ever make it.

QUITLINE Do you *really* want to stop?

CALLER I do.

QUITLINE Tell me any ideas you have about how you could manage the going into the pub situation.

CALLER I'll leave it for a couple of days so that I'm not tempted to smoke. Maybe I'll go in again at the weekend, but I won't drink any alcohol this time. I'll try it a few times on soft drinks and see how I get on. If that seems OK I may be able to drink alcohol later on.

QUITLINE How do you feel about that plan?

CALLER It's worth a try. It's better than thinking it's all or nothing.

QUITLINE You're doing really well, you know. Ring in again after you've been to the pub, and tell us how you got on.

The usual things you associate with smoking can include: having a cup of coffee; the end of a meal; before making a phone call; when you first wake up, as well as many more. The list on page 48, '50 ways to break your habit', has a number of substitutes to try instead. Think of other innovative, silly or surprising ways you can also do things differently for a while. Be as radical as you wish until you are able to reintroduce these elements into your life without worrying that you'll be prompted to smoke.

I knew the mornings were going to be my danger time, because I've always loved that first cigarette of the day, even before I'd made my first coffee. My flatmate at the time wanted to lose weight, so we tackled it together. Her job was to come into my room and haul me out of bed and into my tracksuit before I had time to think. We'd go for an early morning run, and then my job was to keep her running after the first ten minutes, when she'd lose enthusiasm. After a few days I didn't really need to do it, because I'd got over feeling I needed a cigarette first thing. I was doing so well quitting that I'd lost the craving. But I kept it up for her sake, and I

got to enjoy that sense of achievement at the beginning
of the day.

Things that make you feel good about yourself are especially likely to help

CALLER I've called in to thank the counsellor I spoke to last
week. I was a bit all over the place then, and I told him how
impossible giving up seemed to me. I'm pregnant, and I've
been trying to give up ever since I knew, five weeks ago. I
would quit every week. I quit on Monday mornings, and
then I was back to it by the afternoon. We talked about how
I wasn't really feeling connected to this pregnancy, unlike
with my first. I was feeling really guilty about that. You're
supposed to be happy, aren't you? Anyway, he was so nice
and understanding, that I'd like him to know that I've stopped
for three whole days now. The trick that works for me is
that whenever I fancy a fag I sing to the baby instead. They
can hear you know, inside you, and I'm feeling much happier
about it now.

You might want to change your journey to work, if certain
places are associated with buying cigarettes, or where you
usually lunch or hang out afterwards smoking. Instead of
feeling that you're missing out when the other smokers pop
out for a cigarette, take a stroll around the building while
they are lighting up, read the newspaper or phone a friend.
Do something diversionary or active. If you like a cigarette

with colleagues at lunchtime or at the end of a long and stressful day, try to think of something else you can share together, such as a line dancing class or a trip to watch a local non-league football match. When you really think about it you'll find that there are plenty of ways to enjoy being with your friends besides smoking.

Other changes that can help are: varying where you eat your meals at home – at the dining table, rather than on your knee, for instance (if that's when you usually light up); choosing non-smoking restaurants, going to different clubs and other venues, where you have no pleasant memories of having fun and smoking.

It's the kids who seem to have the most trouble changing their routine. I'll suggest going to the library at break, instead of the toilets where the other smokers congregate. Hanging around with non smoking friends – though they usually complain that these are the 'geeks'. It's about finding out where smoking happens, such as secretly at the back of the bus upstairs, and then suggesting an alternative, like sitting right at the front.

You usually have to make most effort to find alternatives when smoking is embedded in the culture of your group, or even your country.

My friends were smoking at high school and I wanted to experiment with it. I'm from Greece and it was fashionable to smoke; most people do, it's perfectly acceptable. As a child it's a way of rebelling, and also showing you are becoming an adult. It seemed linked with being independent and having fun with friends. Then I went to the USA and it was a completely different culture. Smoking seemed to be for very low-class, tacky people. There was no public place where I was allowed to smoke. My American friends said, 'You really need to consider stopping, because here it's not culturally acceptable'. I started to identify with that. It put it in a completely different light. In six months I stopped. I wasn't terribly addicted to smoking, I suppose. It was about having fun and being part of the group – not about stress or calming me down. It wasn't considered fun by my new American friends. I started a very healthy lifestyle and cigarettes didn't figure in it any more.

Gradually you can begin to reintroduce your old routine, and see how you cope with not smoking when you do so. Start to do this fairly early on in the process so that you can get back to normal quite quickly. If you cut yourself off for too long, you may only associate not smoking with the unusual or changed circumstances in which you have been living.

I gave up the first time by going to stay with my sister for a month. It was absolutely brilliant. I suffered a bit with withdrawal, but nothing I couldn't handle. I arrived back home a shining non-smoker, really proud of myself. But then I was back to real life, and I started to crave a cigarette the moment I saw my old friends. I was back to smoking in a couple of days.

Sometimes, though, you might want to make permanent

changes to your life, particularly if smoking for you was connected with a particular lifestyle, or being with a set of people who don't support the changes you'd like to make for a happier life.

My smoking got really bad when my husband left me, and I had to bring up our child alone. I had to give up my teaching job, and I went on the dole. I got in with a particular group of people who didn't work and didn't want to, who didn't see the point in life, and were always complaining – just as I was at the time. We used to hang out together, smoking like chimneys, lounging around on the floor of this woman's room. I've never felt so low – it was like a metaphor for my life: it was down-and-out on the floor. One day I rang the QUITLINE, because I thought I really needed to sort my smoking out. It was eating up a large proportion of my dole money. To my surprise, we didn't just talk about smoking. I found myself telling her everything about my life, and she encouraged me to take a holistic approach. We talked about me eating better, doing exercise, generally looking after myself better. I did all of these things alongside giving up smoking, and I felt like a different person. In fact, I went back into teaching, and severed my connections with the people I'd been hanging out with. They had been dragging me down, and I felt so alive, positive and different, that we had nothing in common any more.

7. No excuses

When you're doing really well at quitting, the moment will come when you feel confident that you'll never go back to smoking. Then comes the danger that you believe you will be able to handle a puff of a cigarette, or just one.

Don't use celebrations or stressful events as an excuse for 'just one'. It'll rarely ever stop there. It does happen, but for most people it only takes a casual cigarette to start them craving for more. There is no such thing as a safe cigarette. You are likely to go back to square one in your struggle to give up, because you renew your body's taste for nicotine.

CALLER I gave up smoking this morning, and now I'm gasping for one.

QUITLINE Tell me what's happening.

CALLER My wife's pregnant, and she's trying to give up. She's cut down to two cigarettes a day. I promised I'd stop as well. I usually smoke 40 roll-ups, most of them at night, because I work nights as a security guard, and there's a lot of hanging round with nothing to do. I've been at work for an hour now, and I'm climbing the walls. I bought some ultra-low cigarettes on my way into work in case I got desperate. At least it's better than my roll-ups, isn't it? If I could smoke just a few like my wife then maybe I could handle it.

QUITLINE Unfortunately it's actually extremely hard to cut out the last few cigarettes. The agony goes on, and you keep thinking about smoking. It can be easier to get it over and done with altogether and give up completely. If you smoke one of those ultra-low ones, you're likely to go right back to smoking.

CALLER So what should I do?

QUITLINE It's up to you. It seems you have three choices –

to give them to someone else, chuck them away or decide to smoke them.

CALLER I've got to do this. I'll bin them.

QUITLINE Do you want to talk about how you're going to cope? (*They go through some strategies together.*)

CALLER I think I'll be all right for tonight, now.

QUITLINE And ring in as often as you like. We're here till nine in the evening.

Although smoking even one cigarette can start your cravings again, all is not lost. In Chapter 5, Staying Stopped, we'll show you how you can cope with a relapse.

8. Treat yourself

It makes sense to reward yourself for doing something so vital to your well-being. You'll be saving a lot of money, so there should be some to spare for a special treat. You can buy regular small treats: a paperback book, a bottle of wine, a magazine or a trip to the cinema – which you can enjoy much more now as most cinemas are smoke-free. Or you can plan for a big treat – something that you save up for and look forward to, such as a holiday or a major household item.

Another good reason for treating yourself is that, in common with most smokers, you might well have used cigarettes as a mini-treat throughout the day, and without this to look forward to you feel bereft. Look back at '50 ways to beat your habit', page 48, for some ideas on this.

CALLER I haven't smoked for two weeks now. I'm six months' pregnant. I think I'm basically over the worst, but it's the evenings I find so difficult.

QUITLINE Why's that?

CALLER I'm tired. I've done everything I have to do, and then I find myself feeling really, really twitchy.

QUITLINE And how would smoking make it better?

CALLER I'd be unwinding, knowing the day was behind me. Feeling I deserved a break.

QUITLINE Sounds as if it would feel like a reward for a day well spent.

CALLER Yes. Or a bit of a treat if the day *hadn't* been that well spent!

QUITLINE So how else could you reward yourself?

CALLER (startled) Pardon?

QUITLINE What other ways could you reward yourself or give yourself a treat at the end of the day?

CALLER I'll have to think about that.

QUITLINE For instance, some people like to get into a scented bath, maybe by candlelight. Or you could ask your husband to give you a massage.

CALLER (amused) He'd like that!

QUITLINE Now that you come to think of it, what other ways could you find to reward yourself? (*They talk about it for a few minutes.*)

CALLER I'd never thought of cigarettes being a reward, or even noticed that I wanted a reward. I've really enjoyed this conversation, it's going to make a lot of difference to me.

9. Be careful what you eat

It's very tempting to substitute food for cigarettes, particularly fast, high-calorie snacks such as chocolate, sweets, crisps or nuts. In common with cigarettes they are an instant treat or reward, and one of the symptoms of withdrawal is feeling hungrier for a time. Some of the desire to smoke is linked to the enjoyment of putting something in your mouth (hence some people use dummy cigarettes or inhalators to help them stop). But snacking on fatty foods or sugar-loaded sweets will also mean that you put on weight unnecessarily. There is usually a weight gain when you stop smoking, but if you pile it on it is because you are eating too much of the wrong things.

Here is a list of ten things to put in your mouth that will do you good, and not put on weight unduly:

1. Sticks or chunks of raw vegetables, such as carrots, cucumber, celery, radishes, tomatoes.
2. Microwaved mushrooms, which are chewy and full of flavour.
3. Pieces or wedges of fruit.
4. Sugar-free gum.
5. Glucose tablets.
6. A handful of raisins.
7. Water from a teated bottle, as used by athletes. The sucking action may help you replace cigarettes, and you can carry one of these bottles wherever you go.
8. Get a cigarette-sized straw (such as a cut-down McDonald's

straw) and put in one of the filters you can buy for roll-up cigarettes, or pack one end with cottonwool. You can draw on this as you would a cigarette.

9. Inter-dental toothpicks, impregnated with toothpaste-like flavour.
10. A cinnamon stick that you can draw on like a cigar – and it looks like one. The smell of cinnamon has been proven to have a feel-good effect on men in particular.

10. Take one day at a time

All that's required of you is to quit for today. Handle whatever comes up, and tomorrow will be easier. Each day without a cigarette is good for your health, your family and your pocket.

Over 30 years ago I was smoking 50 a day, and realised that it was out of control. I thought: *how can I earn enough to pay for my growing family if I get ill?* I was overcome with despair at the enormity of the task. I recognised that in my very stressful job, the time I really needed to smoke was between 4.00 pm and 6.00 pm. However I realised that there were several periods in the day when I didn't smoke or need to – eight hours asleep, 30 minutes in the bath, 10 minutes here and there on the loo, 60 minutes on a motorbike going to and from work, 30 minutes over breakfast, 60 minutes at lunch, and 60 minutes at dinner. Generally, in the early 1960s 'gentlemen' tended not to smoke in the street. So: at least 12 hours when there was no effort needed not to smoke. I reckoned I could just about cope through the day until 4.00 pm, and equally after 6.00 pm until I went to bed. So I managed to kid myself that all I had to do was to give up smoking for only two hours on that day alone. For being so heroic, I determined to reward myself mightily. Better bottles of wine at meals, expensive restaurants, chocolates, lots of theatre (tough to smoke in there), little presents, exciting weekends away with my wife and friends. This made me put on some weight, and cost a lot (but how much would I have spent on fags for 30 years?). It was worth it. The great benefit is being able to taste food more intensively and to smell scents and smells. Your own breath doesn't have that stale smell, which so puts off loved ones. Your clothes only ever carry that pubby smoky smell, if you have been in a smoky pub. My doctor was pleased that I lowered my likelihood of heart attack and stroke in later life. I had been shocked, during my smoking days, to be given a graphic description by a girl of her father's death from lung cancer. She said, 'He either suffocated or drowned – take your choice. It's a horrible death.' Even after 34 years as a non smoker, I don't think I am cured. I have never said that I have given up smoking – only for today! I went for ten years without smoking a thing, then I obtained permission from my life insurance company to smoke three beautiful expensive Cuban cigars a year. It's a wonderfully sensual experience, especially in a trad old gents' club with a glass of port or brandy and lots of good gossipy clubby conversation. As a sixty-one-year-old who feels twenty-five, I know that I did the right thing. My life continues to be hugely fun and interesting and I am fit until whenever my final summons comes.

Chapter Four

Coping with withdrawal

Giving up smoking usually means a period of adjustment. You are saying goodbye to something that has been part of your life, and this takes getting used to. It's to be expected that during the period of withdrawal you will be coping with unfamiliar and sometimes uncomfortable feelings and sensations.

Much is made of what this time of withdrawal might be like, and the focus is often on the more extreme reactions. It's true that for some people it can be acutely painful or miserable for a while, but this is by no means the case for everyone. Many are surprised at the way they can sail through giving up smoking, even if they have smoked heavily for years, simply because they are so determined to kick the habit – and so glad that they have – that any symptoms appear relatively minor obstacles.

It makes sense not to speculate in advance – or to worry

about how it might affect you – but to prepare yourself for the fact that there may well be short-term difficulties. Even if, for a while, these are acute, being well prepared and fully resolved carries you through them.

Day three of giving up I was curled up in the foetal position at university on my hall's kitchen floor with my two friends (40 a day the both of them) laughing at me. I didn't think I'd be able to bear it. I found the best way was to use the energy that giving up gave me. After the first fag-of-the-day-head-rush, smokers generally enter a negative energy cycle. We (non-smokers, that is) can choose to enjoy a positive energy cycle. What I found helpful when I was unbearably restless was to *move*! Jogging is OK for some but bedroom or office boogies are also a buzz. I found my thoughts racing a lot to begin with, and discovered that if I regulated my breathing I regulated my thoughts. I took the five minutes out I would use to smoke a cigarette to pay attention to slowing my breathing down and imagining I was on a beach, smoking a fag, or whatever. Going from smoker to non-smoker is a change in identity and also in behaviour. That means you may have to invest some time in finding new behaviours that give you a kick. The fact is – and this isn't meant to be defeatist but rather realistic – I gave up three times before I last quit (I have now not smoked a cigarette for two and a half years). You have to see each period of giving up as a success not a failure. If you really do want to stop then you will. Just believe that what you are doing is right and you can make the process more comfortable for yourself. We non-smokers are a healthier, happier bunch, so enjoy your new status in life.

For some people the severity of their withdrawal symptoms is enough to make them decide never to go back to smoking.

I gave up when I was pregnant with my first son, nine years ago. I don't remember experiencing problems then – or, at any rate, I didn't know which symptoms were pregnancy ones, and which were because of withdrawal. I didn't smoke for seven years until I broke up with my husband. Suddenly I craved cigarettes again. I went back to smoking and thoroughly enjoyed it. I thought, 'I'll be nice to myself and allow myself to smoke for six months.' But in fact it was three years before I felt able to give up. As a single mother of two boys I felt I should give up, although I loved it. I kept my smoking secret from them, but still managed 20 a day. I was prepared to spend whatever it took to break the habit – to try acupuncture, hypnotherapy and homeopathy. In fact, my homeopath told me that what really mattered was my own resolve and not to waste my money, though she would give me some treatment to help me through. The first day I thought I was going to die. I was shaking, phenomenally irritable, had unbelievable diarrhoea, bad breath, and I broke out in spots. I felt as if I had an awful bug. I started coughing immediately. It felt like asthma, as if I couldn't get any air into my lungs. The next day was just as bad, and I had a headache and felt nauseous as well. I'd reach for my cigarettes while I was working, and they weren't there. I moved my work downstairs to be away from my 'habit' area. After meals I went to my secret place to smoke away from the boys, and think, 'What am I doing here?' I had vivid awful nightmares all night long and kept waking up sweating. The third day was the worst. I burst into tears at least ten times, and I'm usually a cheerful rather than a tearful person! I was coughing up black mucus. The fourth day was so much better, and over the next couple of weeks nearly all of my symptoms rapidly disappeared. In retrospect, I think the homeopathic remedies made me detox much faster than I would have done unaided, which is why the symptoms were initially so severe, but also went so quickly. I'll never smoke again, because I couldn't go through that agony again.

Many people find the build-up to stopping smoking more painful than the decision itself. The worry, the guilt, the subterfuge – all emotional pressures – can feel worse than the purely physical or habitual pangs, which are temporary, and beyond which you can look forward to a happier, healthier, calmer life. Sometimes people who have grappled with these feelings during the build-up are gratified to find that they don't suffer any withdrawal symptoms at all.

The first time I really thought about giving up was when my grand-daughter came to visit me and told me that the teacher had said she mustn't stay in the same room as me when I smoked. That hit hard. I felt terrible about it, and didn't want to harm her. But I didn't stop. I just made sure I didn't smoke when she was around. The next time was when an old friend of mine was dying of lung cancer. The unfair thing was that she'd never smoked in her life. She said to me gently and regretfully, 'How can you keep smoking when you have the choice to improve your health?' That made me feel bad too, but again I just took care not to smoke in her presence. After she died I continued smoking, but with much more guilt and less pleasure. What really did it for me was when I developed a respiratory infection and could hardly walk or breathe. I was on holiday at the time, and the doctor asked me if I smoked. When I said I did, he abruptly replied, 'Well, what's the point of me prescribing you anything then?' That shocked me. I was worried about becoming so disabled that my children would have to look after me. I've always been very independent, and that seemed like a fate worse than death. I gave up then, after 50 years of smoking, and never smoked again. Thankfully, I fully recovered from the infection. And I didn't suffer any withdrawal symptoms at all, so determined was I to maintain my health, and so relieved was I to be free of it at last.

The three kinds of withdrawal

Withdrawal can be separated into three component parts: physical, psychological and emotional, and habitual. The physical is caused by the withdrawal of nicotine, to which your body has become accustomed. The symptoms that have been shown to result from nicotine withdrawal are: depression, anxiety, irritability, restlessness, poor concentration, sleep disturbance and hunger/increased appetite. The psychological and emotional withdrawal depends on what smoking has meant to you in your life, how you have defined yourself as a 'smoker', and how you have used smoking to relieve your feelings in the past. The habitual aspect refers to the sheer mechanical side of smoking, and how it fits into your daily pattern. The psychological, emotional and habitual elements of withdrawal are looked at in most detail in Chapter 2, and they are also briefly examined later in this chapter.

ACTION In your notebook, write down any withdrawal symptoms you have: when they happen, what brought them on, how long they last, and how intense they are. Record your feelings about them. It will help you to focus, and also show you what progress you are making. You'll notice that the episodes become further apart, and the cravings become less strong. This will also help you plan for the difficult moments, and you can use your lists from Chapter 2 to decide how you are going to handle them.

Living without nicotine: physical withdrawal

You face the physical side of withdrawal every day as a smoker. When you wake up in the morning your body has been without nicotine for a few hours, and you may feel your strongest desire to smoke. This is why committed smokers often light up before they have their breakfast, and some before they get out of bed. It may feel like a habit (as it often is) or it may feel like a comfort (psychological/emotional), but it's likely that the first smoke of the day is to stave off physical withdrawal from nicotine. To a lesser degree, you suffer from nicotine withdrawal throughout the day – in between cigarettes – and the longer you can't smoke, the more intense it feels.

The realisation that I was a slave to my smoking came in stages and so did the quitting of the habit. I arranged my life around finding somewhere to smoke; bearing in mind that I could last no longer than an hour before the discomfort and the fidgeting began. I could see no way of managing my life without the dual calming down and pepping up effects of my addiction. When I was on 60 cigarettes a day, I attended a 'stop smoking' group at a local health centre, but I wasn't ready for it, and carried on smoking. However, my body decided to fight for its own freedom three years later. I awoke one morning and tried to have a cigarette but I immediately vomited violently. I tried half an hour later and it happened again. I made attempts at having a cigarette for a day and a half but I was tired out with it all. It was then that I remembered with startling clarity something that the 'stop smoking' group leader had said. She told us that the only thing that was making us crave the next cigarette was the chemical effect of the last one we had just smoked. She had said that if we could make that gap wider and wider, the desire would lessen in intensity. Well, my body had created its own resting space from the toxic smoke and after four days I did not feel the need to pick up a cigarette at all. I had always blamed what I saw as my weak character for not being able to give up smoking but this experience taught me the nature of my addiction to the drug of nicotine.

How nicotine affects your brain

In a technical sense, nicotine withdrawal refers to the loss or drop of nicotine in the blood, and therefore in the brain, as nicotine is carried in the bloodstream through to your brain, where it primarily acts as a stimulant (pepping you up) but can also appear to calm you down. Nicotine changes brain activity through its effects on neurotransmitters and nerve cells in the brain, and appears to change the chemical balance of the brain. Just as importantly, nicotine seems to provoke a chemical process of addiction that is similar to that of other drugs.

Nicotine withdrawal symptoms tend to peak in the first few days after quitting (day three often being particularly bad) and then subside during the following days and weeks. The intensity of withdrawal varies from one person to another but most report that the worst is generally over in three to four weeks. Heavier smokers tend to have more acute symptoms, which is why nicotine replacement therapy (NRT) can help you over the the worst of it.

Recent research suggests that certain smokers may be pre-disposed to nicotine addiction. We now know that there is a gene responsible for metabolising nicotine, and scientists have found that non-smokers are twice as likely to carry a mutation in this gene that helps to rid the body of nicotine. Smokers without this gene mutation are likely to smoke less because nicotine is not so rapidly removed from the brain and bloodstream. By contrast, smokers with the mutated, efficient version of the gene will tend to smoke more heavily to compensate for nicotine being removed more rapidly.

There is another theory that some people find it hard to give up smoking because of the dopamine receptors in their brain. Dopamine stimulates pleasure pathways in the brain, giving us a chemical high every time we eat, drink, or have sex – all elements of survival. When we follow our survival instincts, our brain rewards us with dopamine and we experience pleasure. Nicotine is a chemical that fools the brain into believing it is involved in survival (thus making us feel pleasure), as do alcohol and cocaine. Sadly, of course, all these drugs actually harm our health, making survival less likely.

Recent research suggests that, in the long term, nicotine reduces the ability of the brain to experience pleasure. That means you need greater amounts of nicotine to achieve the same levels of satisfaction. Some people are born with less sensitive dopamine receptors, resulting in chronically low levels. If they start smoking, thus boosting their dopamine, it becomes much harder for them to give up because withdrawing nicotine means their bodies return to the previously low level of dopamine, which means less pleasure.

For these, and other reasons, it is likely that some people are physically more addiction-prone than others. Research shows that there is a real, physical reason why some smokers might find quitting smoking harder than other people. That said, once you have adjusted to living without nicotine, and your brain has become accustomed to doing without the false messages that nicotine send, you will be over the worst. Over the first few weeks the intensity of the craving reduces and over the next few weeks you experience longer gaps between cravings.

What withdrawal feels like

One of the main signs of withdrawal is increased craving. Some people crave cigarettes so much that, for a short while, they can't think of anything else. It can feel as if your body is crying out for a cigarette.

Cravings are usually at their strongest during the first days of giving up. They often peak over a few minutes, and then become weaker. They continue to become weaker after a few days, and the spaces between the cravings gets longer and longer. Although some people report having the occasional craving months or years after stopping smoking, it is never as strong as in the early days, and gradually becomes easier to resist.

Still now, after three and a half years of not smoking, I get the occasional craving. I can only describe it as a sort of hunger in my chest. Now, though, it's a mild, wistful hunger, as in 'I really fancy that!' rather than, as, in the past, when it felt like starvation: 'I have to have it or die!' There are still some moments, such as getting down to work, when I miss it in a different way. Lighting up helped me start. Usually I'll now have a piece of ordinary gum. Taking off the wrapper and putting it in my mouth seems to work. For a while, the worst time was with people with whom I enjoyed smoking, or who were so obviously enjoying it themselves. Now that doesn't bother me at all. About a year ago, something got into me and I felt impelled to pluck a cigarette from a friend's hand and take a long drag of it. I realised at that moment how easy it would be for me to go back to smoking, but, fortunately, I haven't wanted to since.

Physical symptoms

Your body starts to thank you the minute you stop smoking. It cleanses itself of tobacco toxins and within a few weeks you will have a better sense of taste and smell. Your body will also have cleared out a lot of mucus and debris from your lungs. You will be less wheezy and less short of breath. You'll feel fitter and be less likely to become ill. The adverse physical symptoms you may experience before this process is complete are all good signs that the cleansing process is in action, even though they feel uncomfortable at the time.

The following are the main physical symptoms associated with withdrawal. Some people experience none of them or only one or two. It's rare to experience all of them. These symptoms are likely to be most strong in the first week or two after quitting, and are more likely to be experienced by heavier smokers. After four weeks, most of them will have disappeared entirely.

- **Tingling:** You may experience a tingling sensation in your hands and feet. This is because your circulation has improved. The feeling is temporary and will pass.
- **Loss of concentration:** You might find it hard to concentrate. Perhaps you used cigarettes to help you focus. As you give up, you may spend a lot of time thinking about cigarettes and not smoking, which breaks your concentration. But stopping smoking increases the blood flow to the brain, so you'll soon find you can concentrate far more efficiently without cigarettes. Around 60 percent of quitters report this symptom, but it usually lasts a maximum of two weeks.
- **Cough:** It might seem surprising that giving up smoking can cause you to cough more for a while. This is a sign

that the cleansing mechanisms of the lungs are starting to work properly again, and it won't last. Cilia are small hair-like cleaners which line the airways to your lungs. When you smoke, the cilia are paralysed. Once you stop smoking you may start to cough as the cilia begin their work of cleaning out your lungs. Hot drinks, gargling and lozenges may help to reduce phlegm. Drinking lots of water and breathing moist air will also help the cilia do their job.

- **Headaches:** Some ex-smokers experience headaches, which may be caused by increased blood flow to the brain. Withdrawal of any stimulant (nicotine, caffeine) can cause headaches for a short while. They are also an element in detoxing, as the body is becoming accustomed to doing without poisons it had become used to. If headaches persist, painkillers should help but if you're concerned at all about headaches after a few days, or any other physical symptom, see your doctor about it.

- **Constipation:** Constipation in the early days of giving up smoking is caused by the fact that your bowels have come to depend upon the laxative effect of tobacco. This will pass as your body re-adjusts. The usual ways to help with constipation are to eat more fibre, take physical exercise and to drink plenty of fluids. Conversely a few people suffer from diarrhoea as their body detoxes.

- **Change in sleep patterns:** You may find it difficult to sleep or feel more tired and sleepy for a while after quitting. Difficulty in sleeping is largely related to the effects of nicotine withdrawal, and probably the change in your metabolic rate. It may help to have warm milk or a herbal drink before bedtime, or a warm bath. The following simple relaxation exercise can help ready you for sleep.

ACTION Start by concentrating your attention on your toes: tense them and then relax the muscles. Then work your way up your body, tensing and relaxing each group of muscles as you go, finishing with the muscles in your neck and face. The whole process should take five or ten minutes, and will leave your body feeling pleasantly limp and heavy.

Waking at night usually lasts less than a week, and affects about 25 percent of quitters.

- **Sore tongue and mouth ulcers:** These may be caused by the change in the bacteria in your mouth (because you are no longer receiving thousands of toxins from smoke), or by the fact that you may be feeling run down or your immunity may be reduced during the early days of giving up smoking. This can also lead to cold symptoms and sore throat.
- **Dizziness:** Light-headed or dizzy feelings may be due to improved blood supply, with more oxygen, to the brain. This usually lasts less than 48 hours, and affects only 10 percent of quitters.
- **Increased appetite and weight gain:** Many people worry about this aspect of giving up smoking. About 70 percent of people who give up do find that they are hungrier than

usual, and many also find that they put on weight. There are physiological reasons for this, which are explained on page 25. Some experts estimate that smoking one packet of cigarettes a day is as unhealthy as being about 35kg overweight, so the average 4kg weight gain is small in health terms. If you put on more weight than this it is usually because you are using food to substitute or compensate for not smoking, or giving yourself high-calorie treats. Watching what you eat and taking more exercise can combat this problem. This is looked at in more detail in Chapter 5.

If any of these symptoms worry you, or seem particularly severe, consult your doctor. Don't assume that any symptoms you do have are necessarily connected to giving up smoking, and seek help and treatment as you normally would.

Psychological and emotional symptoms of withdrawal

Some ex-smokers experience no physical signs of withdrawal but they do have other difficulties, depending on what smoking has meant to them over the years.

I gave up smoking about four years ago. I was an on-off smoker from when I went to college – a stress and social smoker. I would smoke quite a lot for a few months if I was busy and stressed out, and then hardly at all for a while. It really depended on how I felt and what was happening. I was never convinced that I wanted to stop completely. I liked the whole image of it, and liked being able to have a cigarette with a drink if I was out with friends. But it got to the point where I decided that the effect of on-off smoking was having an impact on my health, whether I wanted to recognise it or not. I didn't smoke for about six months, then started again on holiday with a group of smokers, and continued to smoke on my return. I realised then that it was a myth that I was in control of it. My sister was diagnosed with breast cancer, so I started to think more seriously about health. I was training to be a counsellor, and recognised that, like a lot of people, there were certain situations I didn't know how to deal with in any way but by smoking. I was relying on cigarettes as a way of coping. I stopped smoking half way through training. I was going through a lot of personal development, and I found other ways of dealing with difficult situations. I still kept having the occasional cigarette, though. It wasn't till I decided wholeheartedly that I wanted to stop that I gave up properly. Up until then I thought I 'should' stop, because it wasn't healthy, but I still liked the whole image of it. Sometimes I still do. I think it looks quite glamorous. I still have cravings if I'm out, eating a meal. It's about association: meal, bottle of wine and somebody else lights up and I think 'ooh, yeah!' But I don't do anything about it.

- **Sense of loss, or depression:** Some people describe giving up smoking as like a bereavement. For many, smoking has become such an important part of their daily life and identity that they feel at a loss without it. For some, it feels like the loss of a person – a loved one or friend. You may be very tearful for a while. These feelings pass, and talking about them to someone who understands and won't laugh, such as a QUITLINE counsellor, is particularly helpful. Boredom or loneliness, however, can make the feelings more acute. The more healthy activities you introduce into your life, the quicker you will get over these feelings.

- **Mood swings:** irritability, anger and tension: It's quite common to feel stressed, and therefore irritable, when you first give up smoking, although this rarely lasts longer than about four weeks. Exercise is a good way of reducing tension. It helps the body to manufacture natural opiates – hormones called endorphins – which boost your sense of well-being. Relaxation techniques may also help. It is as well to remember that tension and irritability can be caused by many reasons, not necessarily because you are giving up smoking.

CALLER I need to talk to someone, because I've been so good about giving up smoking, but today I went out with a friend and had two, so I'm scared I'll go back to it.

QUITLINE How long had you not smoked for?

CALLER It's been nearly seven months – just after I found out I was pregnant again.

QUITLINE So you think you're in danger of relapsing?

CALLER Yes, I'm finding it really hard going. My two other children drive me mad sometimes, and I know I'm more short-tempered than usual with them. They're always on at me to play, or they're quarrelling with each other, but I can't bend down, and I can't move so quickly. They're so demanding and I end up shouting at them or crying. I thought all that would be behind me by now.

QUITLINE It should be, after seven months. You're unlikely to be irritable because of nicotine withdrawal now. After all, it's tough looking after two young children when you're pregnant.

CALLER It really is.

QUITLINE What was it like during your other pregnancies at this stage?

CALLER Come to think of it, I've always found this last part difficult.

QUITLINE It could be the hormonal changes, and natural tiredness.

CALLER I think you're right. I was a bit daft and weepy the other times as well.

QUITLINE So going back to smoking won't change your feelings, they're part and parcel of being pregnant.

CALLER That does make me feel better and stronger about not having any more cigarettes. It's normal, I suppose, not about smoking at all.

QUITLINE Let's talk about other ways you can handle it when you're feeling emotional or tense.

ACTION If you're more aware of your anger since you gave up smoking, don't just assume it's a symptom of withdrawal. Examine why you're angry, and if there's a genuine reason for it. How can you deal with it? Is there something you need to do, say, or change that will make the situation easier? If you identify that you're only feeling irritable because you are missing smoking, explain it to your nearest

and dearest and colleagues. Say, 'I'm feeling snappier than
usual because of giving up smoking. Please bear with me.
It's not personal.'

You can help yourself by walking away from situations that
set you off, and remind yourself that the feelings won't last
forever: you won't always be so angry. Other suggestions can
be found in Chapter 2, page 59, and Chapter 5, page 142.

Withdrawing from the habit

Research shows that when former heroin addicts return to
the place where they took the drug, or are simply shown
film of people taking heroin, their brains respond as if they
were taking heroin again. This is known as the Pavlovian
effect – named after Ivan Pavlov, a Russian physiologist, who
discovered he could train his dogs to drool when they thought
they were about to be fed. Before he fed them, Pavlov would
ring a bell. The sound of the bell made his dogs think of food
which triggered saliva production in anticipation.

Much the same thing happens when you are in situations
that are connected in your mind to smoking. If you always
had a cigarette after work, after a meal or with certain friends,
you associate smoking with these activities and for a while
will crave it at these times. The usual advice is to break
these habits first: changing your routine and avoiding certain
situations until you are more securely on the way to quitting
for good.

Changing your routine and the people you see can also

feel like a bereavement. For some, the power of these habits is stronger than the addiction to nicotine. They go back to smoking when they have gone through withdrawal and are symptom-free, having conquered the other cravings, simply because the lure of the habit at certain times proves too much for them.

I started smoking down the local park before I was even a teenager. Most of the time I was on about 20 a day. But when I was about 21 I was off sick after being in a car crash, and I went up to about 100 a day. When I went back to work, where I couldn't smoke, it went down to 40 because it wasn't physically possible to fit any more in. I became a professional giver-upper. I could give up two or three times a day. Then I moved into a house where spores from trees in the back garden brought out my asthma, and after that I wasn't feeling good on smoking. I cut down to four or five a day of other people's. I had friends who were too generous. They kept feeding my habit. Every time I grovelled they'd give me one. I stopped for a few years, but then slowly drifted back into it. I was smoking more and more of other people's, until one day the guys I was working with marched me into a shop and said, 'Your habit's too expensive for us, buy your own!' So I realised I really *was* smoking again and I had to go through all the palaver of giving up once more. I'm one of the lucky people who didn't have a hard time withdrawing from the nicotine, but it was the habit that was the hardest thing. And facing why I was smoking. Why did I have to be one of the group? Was I that weak a person that I needed to hide behind the toilet door with all the other smokers? And I finally found out that I didn't.

Whatever withdrawal symptoms you might be experiencing, you can be absolutely sure that they won't last. How many people do you know who have given up smoking? Most of them will have been through withdrawal and will have come out the other side, as you will if you persist.

Chapter Five

Staying stopped

There comes a time when you have passed through the stage of withdrawal and are out the other side: physically you have beaten the habit, and you are now in a strong position to continue your life as a non-smoker. On average, this takes about a month, although it is quicker for some people, and takes a little longer for others. At around the same time, some people overcome the emotional withdrawal, and stop missing the sheer habit of smoking, although other people find that these symptoms continue for a few more months. After a while you will notice that you have been free of all symptoms – that you scarcely think about smoking from one week to the next – and you become confident that you will be able to remain smoke-free for ever.

Even so, some people relapse after this stage. Some people find it very hard to see themselves as non-smokers, even several months after they've smoked their last cigarette. Insurance companies won't regard you as a non-smoker until you've remained smoke-free for a full 12 months. This chapter helps you to think about staying stopped, and how to cope with the situations that might arise to test your resolve.

Sometimes you are affected by symptoms that seem to be connected to quitting smoking long after it is likely to be the case. You need to evaluate what you are feeling, and whether, in fact, it has anything to do with smoking at all.

CALLER I gave up smoking five months ago. I didn't find it terribly hard. I never had really strong cravings. The worst bit was certain times of the day when I felt low and lethargic, and that's when I always wanted a cigarette. The thing is, that's never really gone away. I would have thought it should be behind me by now. Do you know how long it's going to last, or what I can do about it?

QUITLINE It does sound slightly unusual. Have you had a check-up with your doctor, just in case?

CALLER Yes, and he says there's nothing wrong with me.

QUITLINE So what you're saying is that you have an energy dip at certain regular times of the day.

CALLER Yes. It's at the times when I'd usually smoke – I was never a heavy smoker but those were the times I really felt in need of one. Some days I feel it more than others.

QUITLINE It's an energy dip that you became used to handling by having a cigarette, so you associate it with smoking, which pepped you up for a bit. But it sounds as if those lows occur in you naturally – which means they're not to do with withdrawing from smoking. Perhaps it's a drop in your blood sugar level.

CALLER I do find eating chocolate at those times makes me feel better, but I'm trying not to because of my weight. All I know is that I need a bit of an *oomph*.

QUITLINE Let's look at other things you can do. (*They discussed glucose sweets, herbal teas, vitamin supplements, 'invigorating' aromatherapy oils.*) Knowing that you need that *oomph* at the particular times you've identified, means you can anticipate it and plan for it, rather than wait for the low to hit.

If you felt rather emotional while you were giving up smoking, it can mean that you connect similar feelings to the same cause.

CALLER I'm feeling so tired, and so upset. How long is this going to go on for? I don't know how I'm going to be able to cope with it.

QUITLINE When did you give up smoking?

CALLER It's been nearly seven months now.

QUITLINE You do sound upset, and tired. But after seven months it's unlikely to be because you've given up smoking. What else is happening in your life?

CALLER I've got a lot on my plate. (*She gives a long list of stressful-sounding situations*).

QUITLINE You do have a lot to cope with at the moment. It's not surprising that you feel tired and upset.

CALLER Today's particularly bad. I felt tired like this in the first week after giving up, and one of your QUITLINE lot said that happens when you give up smoking.

QUITLINE That's true, but it passes very quickly. What's different about today?

CALLER Well, it is my mother's birthday. She died two years ago.

QUITLINE You must be thinking about her a lot today.

CALLER I am. She had a hard life.

QUITLINE It's natural to feel tired when you're under stress, and when you're depressed or sad. You're probably still grieving. Get as much rest as you can, and if the tiredness persists, see your doctor about it.

When being a non-smoker becomes normal

It's usually a relief to get to the stage where it feels as natural to be a non-smoker as it did to smoke. A few people, however, miss the fuss that was being made of them while they were giving up. This is especially true if you are still finding avoiding smoking hard at times, yet no one congratulates you any more, or makes allowances for your moods. This can be a testing time, if it bothers you, and for some people it's the point when they start smoking again. When smoking is part of your self-image, it is also difficult to adjust as you find yourself becoming a non-smoker.

CALLER I've given up for three months. I haven't found it difficult, but this is a dangerous time for me. I'm really wanting to smoke now. It's happened to me before. I give up for two or three months and then I break out – go right back to it.

QUITLINE 'Break out' is interesting. Is that what it feels like?

CALLER (laughs) That's me all over. The everlasting wild child, although I'm thirty-two now.

QUITLINE So you've always been like this, not just over smoking?

CALLER I was a good little girl until I was about eleven. Then my mother died and I went to boarding school.

QUITLINE That must have been very difficult for you.

CALLER No, it was great! My dad was really cut up, and it was a relief to be with other kids. (*They continue to talk about this for a while, and suddenly her tone changes.*) I didn't have anyone to put their arms around me – and my mum had just died. I was so lonely and miserable, until I found the way to cheer myself up – I became the most outrageous girl in the class. Then it really was great. I became the centre of attention.

QUITLINE So that's how the wildchild was born? How do you think that's connected to your smoking 'break-outs'?

CALLER How extraordinary. Now you've made the connection for me, I can see I start to feel really uncomfortable about being 'good'. At some level I have to go back to smoking to be me again – the me who's coped by being bad since I was eleven.

QUITLINE So now that you've recognised that, how can you use that knowledge. What are you going to do?

CALLER I'm going to do a *cordon bleu* cookery course.

QUITLINE You've taken me by surprise there! How does that fit in?

CALLER Before my mum died we used to cook together. She was a brilliant cook, and I really used to love it. Somehow, it didn't fit with my image after that.

QUITLINE So it's your way of saying you don't need to be a wild child any more?

CALLER That's right, and that I don't need to smoke.

If you feel your resolve weakening, for this or similar reasons, it's a good time to revisit the lists you made about why you wanted to stop smoking, and the benefits of being a non-smoker. It's also a good moment to see if you can add some more reasons. These are a summary of some that have been mentioned so far, with one or two extras:

- Better all-round health. Stopping smoking reduces the risk of 50 different illnesses and conditions.
- Risk of heart attack drops to the same as a non-smoker three years after quitting.
- Cancer risk drops with every year of not smoking.
- One in two long-term smokers die early and lose on average 16 years of life.
- Setting a good example to your children and to other people's children. You don't want to be a smoking role model, and it'll be easier to convince young people around you not to start smoking if you don't.
- Have much more money to spend on other items. If you saved £2.74 a day, you would have precisely £1000 to spend in a year's time. Given that a packet of 20 cigarettes costs much more than this at the time of writing, and is

going up with every budget, you can see that you will have literally thousands more at your disposal in quite a short time.

- Improved fitness and easier breathing. Just walking up the stairs can be considerably easier. The longer you stay stopped, the more lung capacity you'll have and exercise will be more attractive and enjoyable. Or you'll just find it easier to keep up with small children or walk the dog.
- You improve your chances of having a healthy baby.
- Food and drink taste infinitely better.
- Your skin improves. There is less risk of premature wrinkles.
- Hair and breath smell fresher and sweeter, and so does the house.
- You feel in control of your life, no longer victim to a craving or distracted because you long for a cigarette.
- Travelling is much easier. You have more freedom over where to sit on a train, and since most buses and aeroplanes are smoke-free, these will no longer pose a problem. You will also find it more pleasant to go to the cinema, theatre, restaurants and shops as most forbid smoking.
- Work is more efficient. You won't be interrupted by needing to take smoke breaks, freezing outside in the winter or choking in a tiny smoke-filled smoking room.
- Life and health insurance is cheaper.

When you've been smoke-free for a while, reading about

the health risks associated with smoking can also reconfirm your determination. Indeed, some people only feel able to read about the dangers and the damage smoking does when they are finally getting to grips with quitting. Read through these on page 29.

Dealing with emotions and trigger situations

You are most likely to start smoking again when under some sort of emotional pressure that sends you back to old, comforting habits. People regress in all sorts of ways when times are hard: going for the foods or routines of their childhood that made them feel safe and cared for (for example, a warm drink of milk, a hot-water bottle, particular music, or a shoulder to cry on). Because of the all-purpose, versatile emotional use to which cigarettes are put, for many long-term smokers most major emotional states or situations have connections to smoking. Memories of how you coped in the past will often include lighting up. Even when you've long broken the habit, therefore, and are well over the nicotine addiction, a time may come when you find yourself reacting to pressure by wanting to smoke.

I'd given up fairly easily, and got through a number of difficult situations without feeling in the slightest danger of going back to smoking. But then I had a big presentation to prepare for work, and I couldn't get on with it. The deadline was getting closer and closer and I'd done nothing. I felt paralysed. I started to fear I might lose my job if I couldn't get off my fat behind and do something about it. I thought about those occasions in the past when I'd pulled the rabbit out of the hat after a period of procrastination, and I'd always chain-smoked my way through them, late into the night. So I quite coolly went out and bought myself a carton of 200 cigarettes and started smoking again. I did then begin the preparation, and I did get it done in time. But I know it wasn't the cigarettes, it was the sheer horror of what I was doing to myself, that I had to make it worth it. It took me ages to be ready to stop again.

Strategies to help deal with emotions were looked at in detail in Chapter 2, when you imagined yourself in just those situations in which you'd be likely to want to start smoking again. Those strategies are always available to you. The main emotions – stress, anger, feeling deprived and putting on weight are examined again here.

Stress

Stress is a fact of life, and there will always be periods when you are under more pressure than at other times. As a non-smoker you are, in fact, better equipped to deal with stress – your stress levels are naturally lower than a smoker's, and the healthier your body, the more capable you are of withstanding it. Nonetheless, when you are particularly tense you're not thinking straight, and there is a temptation to reach for a prop you believed served you well in the past.

CALLER I'm at the end of my tether. One of the kids is sick, and I'm up half the night. The lift's not working again, and I have to climb eight floors with two kids, a pushchair and the shopping. I'm worn out. Then when I do manage to get to sleep, the woman above will start vacuuming or putting a load of washing on – really late at night – and these walls are like paper, I can hear every sound. I feel smoking's the only thing that can keep me going. I managed three months, but I bought some cigarettes today. I really don't want to smoke, but I don't think I'm going to be able to stop myself tonight when I'm exhausted and the kid cries.

QUITLINE You think the cigarettes are going to help you, but they won't. You're going to feel bad about yourself, and smoking actually makes you more stressed. What you really need is some help. Someone to take the kids off your hands for a while so you can get some sleep, perhaps during the day. Who could you ask?

CALLER No one! (*Then she thinks about it more, and comes up with some possibilities.*)

When there are situations you can't change, the best way to deal with stress is to build up your health and stamina. Cigarettes, of course, are bad for both. They are a quick fix, which may make you feel momentarily better, but they do nothing for the underlying problem. Effectively tackling stress involves strategies that are not so quick, but their effects are longer lasting.

Ten ways to counteract stress:

1. Eat well. Have a good balanced diet. There are good, healthy options even in instant, convenience meals these

days. Eat plenty of fruit and vegetables, and drink lots of water. Get a good all-purpose vitamin and mineral supplement.

2. Take exercise. It's a good way of winding down, and it strengthens you. See page 92 for some suggestions.

3. Make me-time. However busy you are, set aside some time each day to be alone, and do exactly as you wish, even if it's only taking a leisurely bath. If you have children, bargain with your partner, a friend or neighbour to take them off your hands, and you can do the same for them.

4. Treat yourself. Make a list of things you enjoy, and which help you relax. It may include watching a video, listening to music, talking to a good friend on the phone, gardening, playing a computer game.

5. Say no more often. Don't allow yourself to become over-loaded by taking on too much. When in doubt, give yourself thinking time. Say, 'I'll have to get back to you on that.'

6. Learn to relax. Try the breathing exercises on page 49. Use the money you save by not smoking to pay for classes in meditation, yoga, T'ai Chi, Alexander technique, or on relaxing treatments, such as massage, reflexology, aromatherapy.

7. Ask for support – and give it. Building a mutual support network from friends, family, neighbours, colleagues, members of your religious group or self-help organisations, will mean that you're never alone with a problem.

8. Get professional help. Talk to your doctor, or find a counsellor or therapist who can give you more focused support and let you talk about your problems. Use QUITLINE (0800 002200) and other helplines to take the pressure off at crisis moments.

9. Have a laugh. A good laugh releases tension, and is good for the body. Even in crisis moments and in the midst of tragedy, it's possible to see the funny side of things. Know who to call who can help you lighten up, or watch a favourite funny video.

10. Have a cry. Holding in your emotions contributes to stress. If crying doesn't come easily, help it along with a sad film or book.

I stopped smoking a couple of years ago, after nearly 50 years of 20 to 30 a day. My wife had died, and I had problems with my lungs, caused by working with asbestos for many years, not just smoking. I had a lapse some months after stopping when my niece came to see me and we had an argument. Stress is the difficulty with me. After she left I had a cigarette, and went on smoking for a couple of days. Then I said: 'What am I doing this for? I'm a non-smoker!' That's when I first rang the QUITLINE. We talked about stopping again, but the lady also encouraged me to eat better. She told me to drink lots of orange juice, as it's rich in vitamin C, and I think it's lovely. She gave me lots of ideas for healthier food. I gave the list to my neighbour, who does my shopping for me as I can't get about so well, and she had such a surprise. It's made me feel much better in myself having these things to think about – and I enjoy healthier food. I'll have a banana for breakfast, and something proper for my lunch. I have chewing gum and peppermints instead of chocolate, and I don't feel I'm Mr Blobby anymore.

Uncomfortable emotions

When cigarettes appear to be helping you to cope with your feelings, they are, in reality, masking them. Smokers will often light up when they are feeling disturbed, without ever getting in touch with what the real problem is. Whether it's hunger or sadness or anger, you often neglect to tackle the root cause of it when you turn to smoking instead.

Inevitably, when you're living without smoking, you will become more aware of your uncomfortable emotions, and because you are unused to dealing with them, the idea of smoking to take your attention away from them becomes attractive.

I smoked between the ages of 20 and 25, when the most important thing in my life was love. I remember a cousin of mine, a doctor I was very fond of, said something about what a horrid dirty habit it was, and that got to me more than the health risks at that time. I hated the smell, particularly of my own breath, which I could smell as I breathed out. I'd decide to stop, and succeeded for a while, until something went wrong with the current man. The usual scenario would be me sitting by the phone, willing it to ring. And I'd start imagining him with another girl and get into such a state that all I wanted to do was have a cigarette. It's a drug! It was only when I grew up a bit, and became less adolescent in my reactions that I was able to give up.

The answer is not to go back to smoking, but to understand your own emotional reactions better – particularly when they are prompting you to take action, signs that you might be ignoring.

Anger

While feeling more irritable and touchy is part and parcel of withdrawing from smoking, longer-term anger is usually about things in your life that need changing. Women, particularly, are often frightened of the anger they feel, and worried about losing their temper – especially with their family and children. They may well decide to go back to smoking instead of finding more practical solutions to deal with the source of their anger, or of making requests of people, or changes in their lives. Men tend to worry more about angry feelings if they are going to impact on their work – they are worried about falling out with the boss or colleagues, or of losing their jobs. Often, again, the anger is telling them that changes need to be made, which smoking helps them to avoid.

CALLER I've stopped now for ten weeks, but I'm experiencing incredible mood swings. I'm really scared at how out of control I am at times. I have this sense that I could fly off the handle without warning. I never know when it's going to happen. It's become a huge issue between me and my partner.
QUITLINE Tell me more about what's happening.
CALLER We stopped together initially, but he's gone back to it. I've been crying such a lot. I really hate smoking. I'm so determined, but he does nothing to help. He smokes around me without any apology, or caring how I feel.

QUITLINE Have you asked him not to smoke around you for your sake, at least for a while?

CALLER It's his place, and he says he doesn't see why he shouldn't do what he wants in his own home.

QUITLINE You don't feel able to ask him, because you're not contributing to the costs?

CALLER I'm in no position to insist on anything. He's already so fed up with me that I wonder if our relationship can even survive.

QUITLINE It sounds as if you feel there's an inequality in your relationship, and you don't have any real rights in it.

CALLER I try not to complain about the filth and poison of what he's doing. Smelling him smoking just reminds me of the poison I've been putting into my body all those years, and I can't stand it. Then it builds up in me and I suddenly lose it. We have a terrible row, and sometimes I storm out, go to the pub and get roaring drunk. We've had rows while we've been out, and he just leaves me stranded and drives home.

QUITLINE It sounds as if there are a number of things that need sorting out in your relationship. You're blaming your mood swings on the withdrawal from smoking, when in fact there are some other things going on as well – you don't feel it's your home, you have blazing rows and he drives off and leaves you stranded. It sounds as if the issue of smoking is contributing to what is going on, but it's uncovering anger that is already present. It isn't the cause of it.

One response to going through a period of feeling anger and frustration (sometimes with yourself) is to retreat into tried-and-tested ways of managing it, so that smoking becomes something you contemplate once again, even if you have successfully quit.

ACTION Ask yourself the following question: what needs to change for me not to be angry? Make a list of what needs to be different – behaviour in yourself, behaviour of another person, circumstances to change. Write down one action you can take, however small, that can start this process of change. Taking action is the single most powerful way of turning the energy of anger into a positive force. By choosing your action deliberately, you avoid the unproductive alternative of 'exploding' into aggression, violence, or self-destructive behaviour when it all becomes too much.

Feeling deprived

A generalised feeling of dissatisfaction, when you are bored, lonely, or don't feel that there is much pleasure in your life, is one of the sensations that can make smoking seem attractive to you again. Giving up in itself can provide an interesting focus for a while, as you battle with something that is taking up your attention, but the moment the battle is over can leave you feeling somewhat flat.

CALLER Would you send me an information pack about giving up smoking, please?

QUITLINE Are you planning to give up?

CALLER Oh no, I've given up already. I haven't had a cigarette for a month now.

QUITLINE So is there something concerning you that you'd like to talk about?

CALLER I'm thinking about smoking more than ever now.

QUITLINE What is it about smoking that you miss?

QUITLINE It's the evenings that are the hardest time. I get in, and I think the nicest thing I could do now is have a cigarette. I used to put my feet up and unwind with a glass of wine and two or three cigarettes for an hour.

QUITLINE How have you been coping with this up to now?

CALLER I keep myself busy. I walk in and start cooking. I don't stop. I just keep going all evening, doing various chores until it's bedtime, when I'm completely tired out.

QUITLINE Keeping busy is very effective, and it's something we recommend for the first few days. But for a whole month! You must be worn out! How long do you plan to go on like this?

CALLER I don't know what else to do. I do feel rather frantic but I'm determined to give up. I never thought I'd make it, and I don't want to spoil it now.

QUITLINE What's missing is filling this need you have to relax and unwind at the end of the day. Have you thought of ways of filling that gap differently?

CALLER It seems dangerous to me.

QUITLINE You've done so well by not smoking for a month. You've really got your habit under control. You can afford to experiment with ways of rewarding yourself, getting in some relaxation that won't make you want to start again.

CALLER Like what?

QUITLINE Suppose you had that glass of wine in the bath, where it would be unusual for you to smoke.

CALLER I see what you mean. I hadn't thought I could relax in any other way. (*They continued to talk about various things she would find relaxing.*)

Finding ways to treat yourself continues to be important, even when you are past the acute phase of addiction. If you find yourself feeling flat or deprived in your life as a non-smoker, look back at Chapter 2 for ways that you can fill your time more pleasurably and effectively.

Social pressure

While giving up smoking you might have taken the sensible step of changing your routine, avoiding people and situations that trigger your desire to smoke. Once you feel more confident and in control of your habit you start to resume some of these. This may be the time when you begin to feel vulnerable again, and smoking begins to appeal, as it used to.

Children and teenagers particularly find this hard, as their friends are often more open about applying pressure and attempting to sabotage them. This has been looked at in more detail in the early chapters, and it is worth preparing yourself for the likelihood of this happening by re-reading these sections – when you're going back to school after the holidays, for instance.

YOUNG CALLER School starts again tomorrow, and I know they're going to pick on me for not smoking.

QUITLINE It's something to be proud of, not ashamed.

CALLER You don't know them. They'll *make* me smoke.

QUITLINE No one can physically make you. They can't stick a cigarette in your mouth and make you inhale. What can you do if they insist?

CALLER I could break it in half, or stamp on it. They wouldn't like that.

Adults, too, can find the more subtle pressure from friends, or the atmosphere of certain situations, bring back the desire to smoke more strongly for the moment. Say, for example, you've kept away from all your old smoking haunts for a few weeks, but you're invited to a reunion, or party where you know there will be smokers. Accept that you may be tempted. Beforehand, imagine yourself at this event as a non-smoker. See yourself saying, 'No thanks' to offers of cigarettes. Remind yourself that there are likely to be other non-smokers, or people in the process of quitting, at this event. You can bolster each other's efforts. Two in three smokers want to stop, so it's likely that some of your smoking friends will also be trying to quit.

ACTION Make it a habit to re-read your reasons for quitting before any occasion at which you imagine you might be tempted. Rehearse in advance what you will say or do should temptation arise.

Putting on weight

Women, particularly, can find that they consider starting to smoke again if they have put on weight and are feeling depressed about it. When you're feeling unattractive or out of control about your eating, it can erode your determination to care for your health.

Staying stopped, like quitting in the first place, is determined by your reasons for not smoking being stronger than your desire to smoke. On purely health grounds, it is healthier to be a little overweight – or even quite substantially overweight – than it is to smoke. But these arguments don't always work for you. Sometimes QUIT has calls from people with eating disorders.

CALLER Can you absolutely promise me that I won't put on weight if I stop smoking?

QUITLINE I can't promise that. You might put on some weight to begin with, but if you eat carefully and increase your exercise you should be able to keep it under control.

CALLER If I put on one pound I'll go back to smoking. It's not worth it. I'm half a stone above my ideal weight already and I can't put on any more.

QUITLINE What's your ideal weight?

CALLER Four and a half stone.

The key to maintaining your resolve is to be prepared for a small weight gain, but to be vigilant so that it is no more than that. People who put on a lot of weight have usually not worked out in advance how they are going to manage the increase in hunger, and the craving to put something in their mouth. Women with children complain that they have a lot of sweets around, so that temptation is always there. Others don't question their impulse to reach for chocolate whenever they would normally have had a cigarette.

This is often because when you forego cigarettes you feel that you are depriving yourself. People sometimes say to QUITLINE counsellors, 'I don't want to deprive myself of everything that gives me pleasure.' The answer is to have a balance. Unlike giving up smoking, you don't have to deny yourself completely. If you want a bar of chocolate, plan for it. Have it three times a week, or allow yourself a cream cake when you're out shopping. Being conscious of eating sensibly most of the time will ensure that your weight gain is minor. Increasing the amount you exercise also speeds up your metabolism, ensuring that you burn off any weight faster. Look back at the earlier section for tips in both these areas.

People who diet at the same time as giving up smoking often report that it makes them feel doubly good, but others find the two together hard to do. It can help to plan a strategy to cope with any potential weight gain. For instance, you can make a pact with yourself that for six months you will concentrate on quitting, and when you have conquered that you will tackle your eating habits.

Bear in mind the fact that giving up smoking improves your overall fitness and increases your energy levels. Therefore, if your weight starts to bother you some months into giving up smoking, you are in much better condition than you were before to do something about it. You'll find it much easier than you did when you were a smoker to add exercise into your life, and to have the stamina to build up a good level of fitness. The more active you are, the more you will be able to eat widely, treats and all, without becoming heavier than you would wish.

Dealing with a relapse

Many people stop and start smoking again before they give up for good. Relapsing is part of the process, as this book has shown already. Granted, it's never 'safe' to have one cigarette, or even a puff of someone else's, but you have to keep a sense of proportion. If you think 'I've done it now, so I'm back to smoking again', then it's a self-fulfilling prophecy. The sooner you catch yourself when you relapse, the more likely you are to go on to quit successfully.

CALLER I stopped smoking a week ago using the patches. Last night I got so weepy I thought I was cracking up.

QUITLINE It can be really upsetting to begin with. It's a bit like losing a friend.

CALLER Yes! It's mad isn't it? Do other people feel that, then?

QUITLINE Lots of them. And many people feel weepy. Cigarettes were helping you suppress your emotions before, and now they're coming out.

CALLER That makes me feel more normal. Well, I can tell you now – the kids were playing up and I thought I'd either kill them or kill myself, so I ended up going out and buying a pack and having a few cigarettes.

QUITLINE You've taken several steps forward by stopping for a whole week, and now it's one step back.

CALLER It is only that, isn't it? I can stop again, can't I?

QUITLINE Do you want to?

CALLER Yes, I really do, but I thought I'd blown it. Having my old friend back, as you say.

QUITLINE It's a bit like an adult version of a teddy bear – something to give you comfort at a bad moment. But what kind of friend is it really? Would you want to stay friends with someone who kept taking your money and giving nothing in return, except ruining your health?

CALLER I know one or two people like that! No. I don't. I was doing really well, and I can't believe how much money I've saved already.

Every time you try to stop and every time you relapse you come closer to stopping altogether. Instead of feeling bad about succumbing and beating yourself up for failing, it's much more helpful to look at why you relapsed and see what you can learn from this. Behind every cigarette you smoke, there's a reason that prompted you to do so. Fully understanding those reasons is the key to finding the strategies that will finally help you stop for good.

While you are in the process of quitting you may find yourself dreaming that you've smoked a cigarette. You wake up filled with disappointment, followed by the delicious recognition that you haven't lapsed after all. It's thought that our subconscious minds take a while to catch up with what's happening in our conscious lives. Smoking dreams are an indication that your subconscious is taking time to recognise your new identity as a non-smoker.

The longer you stay stopped, the more likely you are to remain a non-smoker. As the months progress, you'll find new habits and routines have automatically replaced smoking. You'll miss it less and less. Eventually, you'll wonder why you ever smoked and it'll hold no attraction for you.

> **CALLER** I'm ringing in to say thank you. I was calling in all the time when I was first trying to give up, but I haven't called for months now, because I'm not having problems any more. It's five months to the day since I stopped. Do you know, today my husband said how lovely it was to kiss me, because my breath always smells so sweet. I was really touched. Especially because while I was smoking he'd never complained about it, although he's always been a non-smoker himself. I just wish I'd done it sooner.

Successful Quitters
Successful quitters who have won the prestigious Quitter of the Year Award explain how good quitting made them feel.

> 'I set a date for New Year's Day, which was six months away, and asked for nicotine patches for Christmas. Then I put on a £40 bet with odds of 16–1 against staying off cigarettes. I won the bet, which paid for a holiday in Blackpool. The money I've saved from not smoking has helped us pay the mortgage on our new house. I've never been happier.' *Hilda Crawford, from Northern Ireland.*

Karen Griffiths from Wales had tried to quit many times but without success until four years ago, when she announced publicly that she was quitting. 'My confidence has grown enormously since then. I joined a gym and aerobics class, which I loved so much I went on to train as an aerobics teacher. I've got so much energy my friends call me Pentathlon Woman. Life's so much better without cigarettes!'

Bridget Mohan from Coventry quit smoking in the hope that she could donate a kidney for her sister who needed a transplant. Even when Bridget knew she was unable to help she did not restart smoking. 'The disappointment almost made me reach for the cigarettes again. But even if I couldn't help Julie I was determined not to damage my health anymore. I am now totally free from the chronic eczema that's plagued me for years. The skin specialist can't explain why, but I'm drawing my own conclusions!'

Chapter Six

Being a support – helping a smoker to quit

It's hard to stand by and watch people you care about doing something you know is damaging to their health. Many people call QUITLINE because they are frantic with worry about a child, parent, partner or friend who is smoking. They've usually tried everything to make them stop: nagging, cajoling, scaring them, offering bribes and rewards, or making threats. They want QUITLINE to give them the magic formula to help the smoker stop.

It's hard to hear the truth, which is that until a smoker wants to stop for his or her own reasons there is no way you can force or persuade them to. That said, however, you can take action. You can offer them support at all stages: you can show understanding when they feel 'hopelessly' addicted; you can help them ready themselves when they are thinking about stopping; you can cheer them on through the early days of giving up, and continue to offer support should they find the going becoming tough later, or if they relapse. By being a support you increase their chances of quitting successfully.

It's also essential to recognise that what you *don't* do is as important as what you do. Putting pressure on smokers, even though you are doing it for the best reasons, is counter-productive. As the majority of smokers believe that smoking helps them with stress, pressure from you is likely to make them want to smoke more rather than less. That doesn't mean you shouldn't agree rules about where and when they smoke around you, around your children, or in the house, but it does mean that anger and complaints will delay the result you want.

My son's at university, and smokes along with the rest of his friends. I'm very worried about it, obviously. As a QUITLINE counsellor I probably know better than most what he's doing to his health. Equally, I know that putting pressure on him won't work. The other night we went together to see a friend of mine. She smokes, and was complaining about a health problem. In a casual way I touched on the benefits of giving up: about detoxing, about feeling good, the kinds of exercise that would help her – how great it is to quit when you only have minor health problems which will soon clear up if you stop. I mentioned the smoking cessation group I run, which is attended by people who don't want to give up but have life-threatening illnesses. I work with groups of 10 or 12 over a six-week period and if only two stop that's good news. In the first two weeks five usually drop out. It's a shame that they have to get to the point where their lives are in danger, and even then they're so heavily addicted that they can't quit. My son was listening, and he takes it all in, but I would never lecture him directly. Children always want to do the opposite of what you say! He's said to me, 'Mum, I don't want to give up just yet.' The fact that he says 'just yet' shows me that it's in his mind, and I trust he will give up sooner rather than later.

Before they are ready

Before the smoker has decided to stop, the best thing you can do is to make your concern known, while also understanding what it's like to be in the grip of a habit that you believe you can't control. Given that around 70 percent of adult smokers want to stop smoking, it's likely that the person you're concerned about also wants to stop, even if he or she doesn't currently feel able or ready. Fewer children and teenagers are as worried about their own smoking, but the numbers who call QUITLINE demonstrate that, for all their bravado, many would like to give up. People who want to give up smoking, yet can't, are already feeling bad about themselves, so being heavy-handed in your criticism is likely to make them feel worse.

> **YOUNG CALLER** I'm really worried about my dad. He smokes so much and coughs all the time. I'm frightened he's going to die. How can I make him stop smoking?
> **QUITLINE** Does your dad want to stop?
> **CALLER** No he doesn't, he tells me there's nothing wrong with him.

QUITLINE You could give him this number and suggests he calls us.

CALLER He wouldn't do that.

QUITLINE Would you like me to send you an information pack about giving up smoking, which you can read through together?

CALLER He wouldn't want to do that either. Isn't there something I can do?

QUITLINE There's nothing you can do to actually force him to stop. How do you feel when your dad and mum tell you not to do something you really want to do and they nag you?

CALLER I feel a bit upset and angry at them.

QUITLINE Do you ever do it anyway?

CALLER Sometimes, when they won't find out.

QUITLINE That's a bit like how your dad is feeling. What you can do is tell him how worried you are about him smoking, and that it's because you love him. He might change his mind about smoking, and if he does you can tell him that we'll give him lots of help if he'd like.

It's important to understand how hard it can be for some smokers even to contemplate quitting. If you've never smoked yourself, read through the earlier chapters aimed at smokers to give yourself a sense of what smoking may mean to them. Even if you used to smoke, your reasons might have been very different from the person you're currently worried about, or you might have been less dependent. Rather than nag or preach about the health dangers, therefore, it is much more useful to ask what smoking means to them, what they like about it, when they find it helps, and what they would miss if they weren't smoking.

ACTION If the smoker is willing, say you'd like to understand better why they continue to smoke. Make it clear that you are not going to use what they say as an excuse for a lecture, but that you'd like to see things from their point of view. If they've never thought about it before, prompt them, 'What do you like about it?' 'How does it help you?' 'Which cigarettes do you most need?' Don't argue with what they say, even if it sounds strange or wrong to you, and don't come up with things they could do instead of smoking. Just listen. If you want to say anything at all, repeat back what they've told you: 'So you're saying you need a cigarette when you feel stressed?', 'You really enjoy smoking after a meal'. The point of this exercise is not to make them want to give up, but to give you the information you need to understand them better.

Understanding why they smoke won't make you stop worrying, but it can help you accept that they can't quit just because it's the right thing to do. What do you do every day that gives you pleasure or keeps you going, and how easy would it be for you to stop it? Do you drink tea, coffee or alcohol? Do you have a sweet tooth and a craving for sweets or chocolate? Do you over-eat on other snack foods? Must you watch certain programmes on TV? Do you play computer games? How would you feel, if every time you put the kettle on, reached for a sweet, changed the channel, or switched on your computer, someone complained, tried to stop you, said that you should never do it ever again, or gave you a long lecture about why you shouldn't? You'd likely feel resentful at the very least, even if you knew it was for your own good.

The good news is that being understanding, and not interfering makes others far more likely to entertain the idea of giving up at some stage, even if not just yet. They feel supported by you, and not judged harshly. They'll also be more prepared to hear what you say on the subject when it is not a constant reproof. People who are regularly nagged or criticised close down. They don't really listen, and what you say washes over their heads.

CALLER My boyfriend is driving me mad with his smoking. We argue about it every day.

QUITLINE Does he want to give up?

CALLER He says he does. I get all these promises, but he never does anything about it. I say, 'Here we go again . . . So much for your good intentions', and he just sits there blowing this disgusting, smelly smoke all over everywhere.

QUITLINE The fact that he says he wants to give up is a good sign. Many people have good intentions, but take time to be ready. You want to help him, but perhaps you're putting too much pressure on him at the moment.

CALLER He'll never stop if I don't.

QUITLINE Do the things you say result in him not smoking, or telling you that he feels more positive about stopping?

CALLER Well, now you mention it, no. He often gets his

jacket and storms out and says he'll go the pub where he can smoke in peace.

QUITLINE Why does he continue smoking?

CALLER I haven't a clue! Why would anyone? I think he does it just to spite me.

QUITLINE Why don't you discover why he finds it so hard to stop? How about *not* trying to persuade him for a while, and see what difference that makes?

QUITLINE hears from smokers who say their desire to give up is impeded by pressure from people around them. Comments such as, 'You don't really want that cigarette' drive them crazy, as do tactics such as hiding or throwing away their cigarettes. Often hearing about the health risks makes them feel that they've done so much damage to themselves already that they might as well continue. Some of them feel unbearably guilty when they know their loved ones are suffering for them, but it can make them want to smoke more.

CALLER I've got to give up for my son's sake. He's only got me. This morning he took the packet out of my hand and threw it at the wall saying, 'Mummy I don't want you to die.' He's six years old.

QUITLINE And how do you feel about that?

CALLER Well, obviously I can't bear it that he's upset. And of course I don't want to die. Who'd look after him? But I'm not going to die. I've tried cutting down when he's around, but as soon as he's in bed I virtually chain smoke.

Patience and tolerance are needed when you're around a

smoker who is not ready to give up. QUITLINE (0800 002200) can help you there. Some people call when they are really annoyed with a smoker, or feel at the end of their tether. Talking to a counsellor for a few minutes is more productive than starting an argument with the smoker.

If you remember your own struggles to give up smoking (or to give up anything else), you might find it in yourself to be more patient. But ex-smokers can sometimes be the most intolerant. Having conquered it yourself you don't see why others shouldn't be able to. Be assured: your example is more useful than anything you can say. Knowing that you've given up – and survived happily – is the most effective advertisement for non-smoking, and in time it will have its effect.

Conversely, of course, you will be even less successful in trying to persuade someone not to smoke if you are a smoker. This is more common than you might think. Usually it's parents who try to stop their children smoking, while continuing to smoke themselves, or the partner of a pregnant woman, or the relatives of someone who has been diagnosed with a smoking-related illness. The most effective thing you can do in these cases is offer to give up alongside them, or give up yourself even if they insist they won't or are not ready.

If you've never smoked yourself, the person you're trying to help may say at some point that you've no idea what you're talking about. Rather than be provoked, you can respond pleasantly, 'Yes it's true I don't know what it's like. So why don't you tell me?' Invite them to open up to you, to tell you how they're feeling.

Living with a smoker

Just because you can't make someone give up smoking doesn't mean that you have to put up with them smoking around you, your children, or in the house, if you don't want to. If you're worried about your own health and the implications of passive smoking, or you don't want to sanction your children's smoking by allowing them to do it at home (even if you smoke yourself), or if you just don't like the way it makes the place smell, you are entitled to draw up some rules. This will be much more successful if the rules are made in conjunction and with the agreement of the smoker. Most smokers will understand the fairness of this and agree to it, even if they don't like it. Some are relieved to have rules which cause them to cut down. The drawback is that rules make some smokers rebellious, and more determined than ever to continue smoking.

Supporting a quitter

I supported my husband through giving up smoking. We set up a system of rewards – four weekly ones covering the first month, lots of monthly ones and an annual one, some of which was to be paid out of the money saved. We've just passed the one year point and there have only been two lapses – both of only one cigarette. Two other things helped. We scheduled the first really awful ten days for when we were on holiday lazing around in France, and he allowed himself to have as many nicotine chewing

gum pieces as he wanted. He didn't need any after a
month or two.

Once a smoker has decided to give up, and the quitting day
has dawned, you can give more active support. This means
being a cheerleader, rather than a policeman. Most people
need acknowledgement of how they're doing, and what an
achievement it is.

I tell callers to the QUITLINE to let the quitter know how proud of
them they are. Give the person a hug and say, 'You're doing
really well, and I know it's hard.' Bring home a bunch of flowers
in acknowledgement of the fact that they can experience scents
better after only a short time of giving up. Little things that make
them realise that someone is thinking about how well they're doing
and celebrating it. Kids can get involved as well, saying, 'Well
done mum!' and can make a star chart.

One nice thing to do is celebrate the milestones during
the first few days of quitting. If you don't use nicotine
replacements, your body is free of nicotine after 48 hours.
The quitter might appreciate you marking this with a small
celebration, or simply by mentioning it, even if he or she hasn't
remembered it. This is the time that the sense of smell and taste
improve, so a meal or a foodie treat might be appreciated, or
a scented candle, some perfume or aftershave. Some people
tuck notes of congratulation into a lunchbox, a handbag, or
a pocket, for the quitter to find as the days progress. It's also

an idea to make a small ceremony each day of putting the money saved into a jar. Some supporters match the quitter's own contribution with some money of their own, so there is double the amount. It can also help to be appreciative about how much pleasanter the quitter is to kiss or cuddle, and to mention how nice-smelling they are.

YOUNG CALLER My mum's trying really hard to stop smoking, and I wish she would. It's ever since my dad left that she smokes more. Sometimes I think she's stopped because she hasn't done it for a whole day. But then she starts smoking again.

QUITLINE If you ever notice that she's not smoking do something really loving, like making her a cup of tea, or put your arms round her and give her a cuddle and a kiss, and let her know that she's cared for.

Stressing how well the quitter is doing is important. Say you appreciate how hard it is, and how well they're doing to have come so far. You can help by reminding them of the reasons they want to stop smoking.

It is worth checking with the quitter whether support of this kind is helpful for them and, if not, what would be. Some people find it better not to have any attention drawn to their efforts to give up, because it makes them feel more pressured. Respect their wishes, and take a back seat if this is more welcome.

ACTION Ask how best you can support the quitter in his or her resolve. Make a list together before quit day, so that you can then do the agreed things on your own initiative.

Supporting long term

Giving up smoking is a process and people may need your forbearance for a time. While some people sail through it fairly easily with little in the way of withdrawal symptoms and without mood swings, other people find it more challenging. They may be very much more emotional. They miss the 'companionship' of smoking, and may grieve for a while, becoming rather tearful or depressed. This is when they'll often appreciate your sympathy, and anything you can do to cheer them up and take their mind off it.

More difficult to deal with is the irritability or downright anger that some quitters feel and express as they are going through withdrawal. It helps everyone to know that this is just a phase, and a fairly normal part of the process. You need to be especially patient at this time, and help to take the pressure off in any way that you can.

Mothers often say evenings are the worst. They call QUITLINE and complain, 'The kids are really getting on my nerves and I feel I really, really want to smoke. I get so irritated with them, and then feel guilty because I'm so irritable.' They often think it would be better for everybody if they went back to smoking. That's when the partner needs to come in and take charge. Mum needs to be allowed to put her feet up, relax, and have some space.

At worst, some people become so intolerable that family

members and friends are inclined to beg them to start smoking again so that peace can reign once more. Don't be tempted to do this. Nicotine withdrawal does not last long. They should be over the worst of it quite quickly. However, irritable behaviour: snapping, tongue lashing, banging doors and mood swings may continue for a few weeks. It's not just the physical addiction they're missing. It's the psychological one too. Changing habits is stressful, and some people react to stress by becoming angry, particularly if they've always coped with similar feelings before by lighting up. Remember it's the addiction talking, not the person.

What helps most people through this stage is taking more exercise. It's an excellent way to work off pent-up feelings. You might want to try taking up a sport or hobby together – something you'll both enjoy. Short bursts of vigorous exercise, even if it's only a quick run round the block, can be a good way to transform the irritable feelings into a sense of achievement.

Supporting a quitter who has relapsed

You might find your patience wearing thin when someone has successfully quit for a while and then gone back to it. Many people quit a few times before they finally give up for good. Remind the smoker of that, and remind yourself.

The same applies, however: you still shouldn't pressurise or nag, though it is often tempting to do so. Now, indeed, you might feel you have extra ammunition – perhaps if you keep drawing their attention to how they succeeded before you will bring back their resolve. In fact, the opposite is the case. Their sense of failure may well increase. They have to find their own new resolve again, in their own time.

Most people need to know that you love them whether or not they smoke. Their self-esteem is likely to have suffered when they went back to smoking, and the lower your self-esteem, the harder it is to quit.

What you can do, if they are willing to be helped, is to find out why they felt they had to start smoking again. This knowledge will help them the next time around. Suggest they talk to a QUITLINE counsellor about this: by now they will have got the message that QUITLINE will not judge, criticise or coerce, but will simply help them to understand themselves better.

Supporting a quitter when you still smoke yourself

CALLER Is it right that you don't think someone should go on and on at someone else to stop smoking?

QUITLINE That's right. It doesn't seem to work.

CALLER OK. I know I'm pregnant and he's not, but it's a bit rich for him to tell me to stop as if it's the easiest thing in the world, when he's still doing it, isn't it?

QUITLINE It sounds as if it's making you angry.

CALLER Furious.

QUITLINE Perhaps you can explain to him why it's not helping.

CALLER No – *you* do it! Here he is! (*She thrusts the phone at her partner.*)

It is more complicated to offer support to someone who's giving up if you continue to smoke yourself. But that doesn't mean it can't be done nor that you shouldn't try. Firstly, don't feel guilty that you aren't giving up, too. You have to make your own decision. But don't try to bully them into it if you're not giving up yourself, even if you intend to. You're in a weak position if you smoke yourself, and they'll take even less kindly to pressure from you.

Instead, ask how you can help. Make it clear that although you smoke, you can still support them. You might, in fact, be the very best person to support, because you know how necessary smoking is to you, or how enjoyable you find it.

Respect the fact that they might prefer you not to smoke in their presence, at least at the beginning, and make this effort for them. This is likely to be partly because they cannot bear to be around temptation and partly because they don't want reminding of what they're missing; or they might find cigarette smoke intolerable and physically irritating. One of the biggest hurdles someone giving up smoking faces is being around other smokers, which is why QUIT usually recommends a change in routine to avoid smokers for a while.

Some ex-smokers, however, enjoy a vicarious thrill in watching you smoke. They may love being around the paraphernalia of smoking: the smell, the packets, the ashtrays, the dog ends.

When they are tempted to smoke

The time may well come when the quitter's resolve falters and the desire to smoke becomes strong. This can happen because of the usual cravings, or because they believe they've beaten the habit, and one cigarette or one puff won't matter. In fact, one puff is sometimes all it takes to become a smoker again, if not immediately, then in the days that follow. You might feel that you are being kind by giving them a cigarette, or a drag of yours, but you are helping them to undo all the good work they've done so far. If they've told you they want to stop, and they've asked for your support, honour and respect this. At those moments you may be required to be the strong one. Bear in mind that the intense craving to smoke rarely lasts longer than five minutes. Help them resist the temptation for those few minutes and they may well find their resolve coming back as good as ever.

Do you really want them to succeed?

When you smoke yourself, you might be ambivalent about a friend or loved-one giving up. You might feel it changes your relationship, or it makes you feel worse about your own habit. Recognise these feelings, and understand that, because of them, you might not be able to give whole-hearted support. Be especially vigilant that you don't subtly encourage them to go back to smoking. It's much better to explain your feelings of doubt openly, than to sabotage indirectly. Then you can both decide how you are going to handle the situation.

Quitting together

The best use you can make of these feelings is to use the opportunity to give up as well. Remember, though, that you have to have good reasons of your own for wanting to stop, or you're unlikely to stay the course. Use the other chapters in this book to decide whether you are ready, and how you will plan to stop.

Being a support to someone who's giving up smoking, whether you smoke yourself or not, can test your patience at times, especially if the quitter is finding it hard. If necessary, find some support yourself – either by calling Quitline, or from a friend who'll hear you out. Read the chapter on withdrawal to help you understand it better, and so that you can be reassured that the difficult behaviour or mood swings won't last. Once the smoker has stopped for good, you'll get your thanks – and if you were very worried, you won't even need to be thanked.

A little boy phoned up and said, 'One of your Quit people came to my school and talked about smoking. She gave me a postcard about it, and I gave it to my mum. She didn't read it then. But she put it on the fridge and she read it later. She's stopped smoking now, and I'm just phoning to tell you that I'm really, really happy.'

Chapter Seven

What works?
How to find the quitting method that works for you

Of the millions of ex-smokers in the UK, three out of four were able to give up without any special help. Wanting to stop is clearly the single most important factor in successful quitting.

I decided that it was time for me to give up – I was desperate to – so I went into the chemist to look at all the products that could help me. One of them had the selling line that said, 'I smoke because I like it. I also want to stop.' It jumped out at me. I can hardly explain the amazing impact that it had. The fact that it was recognised that you could really enjoy it *and* want to give up was mind-blowing. I was a seriously addicted chain smoker, yet for some reason, for which I thank heaven, that acknowledgement of what I felt had such a profound and liberating effect that I walked out of the chemist without buying anything, and never smoked again.

Nowadays many people recognise that quitting can be difficult and some people need extra help to deal with the cravings and the dependency. It is only in the relatively recent past that any help has become available. QUIT has evaluated the evidence on all the available products and methods to see which are the most effective. The following guide will help you choose which to try. It may take trial and error to find the one that suits you best. Many successful quitters try a variety of methods before they find one that helps them most, and many ex-smokers relapsed before finding the way that helped them to stay stopped.

I used several aids when giving up; from fiddling with toothpicks to chewing liquorice sticks (those bits of woody twig you can buy in health food stores). Those substitute occupations helped relieve the psychological symptoms of addiction. I haven't smoked for three years now, after being a smoker for over 40 years.

The important point to bear in mind is that no method can do it for you, however good, unless you are ready, and really want to stop for reasons that motivate you. This is because addiction to smoking is complex. There is the physical addiction to nicotine, from which some smoking cessation aids help you withdraw. Then there is the habit, as well as the psychological and emotional reasons behind your desire to smoke, which can make giving up so hard. These are looked at in more detail throughout the rest of the book, so if you have turned to this chapter first go through the earlier sections and read about the other elements of addiction.

You need to know which aspects of smoking are important or pleasurable to you so that you can protect yourself from failure and disappointment. If, for instance, you expect nicotine replacement therapy or acupuncture to cure you completely without experiencing any difficulties you won't be prepared for the quite normal cravings every quitter experiences sooner or later.

CALLER (*angry*) The quack tells me my lungs are shot to pieces and I've got to give up smoking. He gave me your number and told me to ring you. So what can you do about it?

QUITLINE Tell me more about why you want to give up.

CALLER What's there to say? He says if I don't give up I'll die. It's not as if I haven't tried.

QUITLINE What did you do before, and why didn't it work?

CALLER What didn't I try? (*He reels off all the smoking cessation products and alternative therapies he's used.*) It's all a con and a waste of money. When I pay my money I expect results.

QUITLINE It sounds as if you're looking at these things as a magic wand. None of them is going to be able to guarantee that you're never going to want to smoke any more. They are 50 percent of the process, the other 50 percent comes from you. You have to want to give up.

CALLER Well you're no bloody use either. As I suspected

– a waste of tax-payers' money. (*He slams the phone down.*)

Nicotine replacement therapy (NRT)

Nicotine replacement therapy relieves the symptoms of withdrawal from the physical addiction to nicotine by introducing into your system some of the nicotine you used to get from smoking. Clinical trials have shown that, used correctly, they will double your chances of success. If you smoke your first cigarette within 30 minutes of waking, you are likely to benefit more from higher dosage NRT. Very light smokers (who smoke fewer than 10 cigarettes a day), or people who don't inhale, may not need them.

You may still experience a craving to smoke, because you miss your habit, or because you have become used to smoking to help you through certain situations. NRT therefore works best when you are using tactics to combat these other factors, or are combining it with counselling or another form of support. Some NRT products offer a support package as well. These vary from a free telephone number to a personally tailored plan suitable for each user. NRT is by far the most thoroughly evaluated treatment for tobacco dependency and the conclusion drawn from these studies is that it helps smokers to stop smoking in both the short and long term. The rates for staying stopped remain high. Trials do not show a marked difference between the brands.

NRT is much safer than smoking, because it does not contain any tar or carbon monoxide, which cause most of the ill-health consequences of smoking. One advantage of NRT is that you are not taking a new drug, but are simply taking a familiar one (nicotine) in its clean form and in lower doses than while smoking. Check with your doctor or chemist if you are not sure whether it is right for you.

Which method of NRT will work best for you?

There are four different ways of getting nicotine through NRT: patches which work through the skin, lozenges, tablets and gum which are taken through the lining of the mouth, the inhalator which mimics the action of smoking, and the nasal spray which is taken through the nose. Personal preferences and price will be considerations that influence your choice, but think about the psychological aspect, too. For example, do you feel the need to put something into your mouth or to inhale? If so, you may prefer gum, lozenges or the inhalator, as they give you something to do, and you can regulate your nicotine fix when the craving is strongest. If you smoke steadily throughout the day, the patch may suit you better. If you smoke mainly in response to cravings or stress, the other methods might be more flexible for you.

Nicotine gum (Nicorette, Nicotinell and Boots)

You can buy the gum over the counter from the chemist, and don't need a prescription. It comes in two strengths: 2mg for lighter smokers and higher-dosage 4mg pieces. One piece should be chewed slowly for 30 minutes when the urge to smoke occurs. If you find yourself chewing more than 15 pieces of the 2mg strength over 24 hours then you probably need the higher dosage. The 4mg dosage has been shown to be more effective in people who typically smoke at least 15 cigarettes per day.

You need to keep the gum in your mouth for the full half hour. You should not chew constantly throughout this time. You can expect it to taste rather peppery. When you are not chewing, rest it between your gum and the side of your mouth. The nicotine is slowly absorbed through the lining of your mouth, not by swallowing. Swallowing saliva while chewing, or drinking (for example tea, coffee, cola), reduces the effectiveness.

Gum can be especially useful if you miss putting something in your mouth when you give up smoking. You are less likely to snack instead. A very small number of smokers transfer their nicotine dependence from cigarettes to the gum.

> I gave up with the gum. I bought myself a beautiful silver cigarette case from a junk shop and kept my supplies in it. It was three years before I felt confident enough to stop buying it. Even so, I carried the case with the gum in it around for some months afterwards. Then, one day I gave it as a present to a friend who had just stopped smoking, and I knew I was cured.

- *Usage:* about three months.
- *Possible side-effects:* irritation of the mouth and throat, which lessens with use. Mild jaw ache, indigestion (particularly if you chew too vigorously), nausea.
- *Other considerations:* chewing may be uncomfortable if you have dentures. It is not advisable to use it if you suffer from stomach ulcers.

- *Effectiveness:* trials show gum can double your success rate.

Nicotine lozenges (Nicotinell)

Some people do not like chewing gum or are in situations where chewing might not be acceptable. Lozenges are supposed to be gently sucked until the taste becomes strong (rather than chewed) and then kept between your gum and the lining of your mouth, through which the nicotine is absorbed. When the taste fades, start sucking again. The nicotine is absorbed through the lining of your mouth, so sucking harder, chewing and swallowing will make the lozenges less effective. The nicotine is slowly released over 30 minutes.

- *Usage:* a maximum of 25 lozenges in a 24-hour period. Each lozenge is equivalent to one piece of the lower-dosage gum. It is suggested that you have as many as you want, up to the maximum dose, for the first eight weeks, reducing to half in the following two weeks and continuing to reduce to zero.
- *Possible side-effects:* nausea, otherwise similar to other products.
- *Effectiveness:* as with gum. Will double the success rates compared with placebo or no lozenge.

Nicotine tablets (Nicorette Microtab)

You place one tablet, which is about the same size as a sugar-substitute sweetener, under your tongue, and let it dissolve slowly at its own rate, without sucking. The nicotine is absorbed through the lining of your mouth. It is a particularly discreet method.

- *Usage:* you are allowed a maximum of 40 tablets in a 24-hour period. If you smoke fewer than 20 cigarettes a day, one tablet per hour should be enough. If you smoke more than that, you can use two tablets an hour.
- *Possible side-effects:* same as for gum and lozenges.
- *Effectiveness:* clinical trials demonstrate that in common with other NRT methods, the Microtab doubles your chances of success.

Nicotine patches (Nicorette, Nicotinell, NiQuitin CQ and Boots)

CALLER How much will patches cost me?

QUITLINE (*mentions current price.*)

CALLER What? I'm not spending that amount of money!

QUITLINE You've already told me that you're smoking at least a couple of packets a day – that's over 14 a week. The most expensive patches cost roughly the equivalent of five packets a week. You'll be saving money.

CALLER I've never thought how much I spend before. When you put it like that it sounds better, but it's still a hell of lot to spend out in one go. It had better work!

QUITLINE Think about it: you'll be spending that money for three months. If you go on smoking you'll be spending what you do now – and more – for the rest of your life!

A nicotine skin patch looks like a sticking plaster, which you put on to an area of dry, non-hairy skin, usually on your upper arm. The patches come in varying strengths, depending on how much you smoke, and your level of dependency. Each patch lasts either 16 or 24 hours. The nicotine is slowly absorbed through your skin so that you have a continual supply of nicotine, which should help prevent the cravings that are purely physical. Even if you do feel like smoking, the urge won't be as strong. There is no rapid rise in nicotine concentration in the blood, so you don't get the quick fix of other methods.

- *Usage:* up to three months.
- *Possible side-effects:* itching, redness of the skin, or mild rash. You can avoid these by changing the position of each new patch. It may also cause vivid dreams or disturbed sleep when worn overnight.
- *Effectiveness:* patches can double your chance of quitting.

When I talk to people who say that patches haven't worked for them, it often turns out that they haven't been using them correctly. They think it's too expensive so they stop using them after the first week, or well before the three months is up. Or they'll keep a patch on for two days, to make it last longer – and of course they're not getting any nicotine from it on the second day. Some of them get a craving to smoke, take the patch off and light up a fag, and then put it back on again. Then they wonder why they're having so much trouble and blame the patches for not working.

Inhalator (Nicorette and Boots)

The inhalator looks like a cigarette holder and contains a nicotine cartridge. You get the nicotine by puffing on it, as you would on a cigarette, or by taking shallow puffs, as you might if you were a pipe-smoker. But unlike with smoking, the nicotine is absorbed through the lining of the mouth, rather than carried into your lungs. You absorb the same amount of nicotine whether you inhale deeply or shallowly. It is most appreciated by people who miss the hand-to-mouth action of smoking, but it means that you don't break the habitual connection between relief from craving and inhaling, and some people become dependent on them.

- *Usage:* each cartridge contains enough for three or four 20-minute puffing sessions. Suggested use is for six months. For the first eight weeks use 6–12 cartridges a day, for the next two weeks reduce by half, then reduce each week after that until zero. Best used at room temperature.
- *Possible side-effects:* usually few. Similar to other products, plus mild cough.
- *Effectiveness:* can double success rate.

Nasal spray (Nicorette)

Nasal spray comes in a bottle, similar to nasal decongestants.

You put it in your nostril and squirt, administering a fine spray of nicotine. It is a particularly quick and efficient way of getting nicotine. The absorption through the lining of the nose is fast – you feel the nicotine hit more quickly than with other methods.

- *Usage:* recommended only for three months. You can use it when needed, to a maximum of one spray to each nostril twice an hour. The suggested pattern is to use for eight weeks as required up to this dose, reducing by half in the next two weeks and continuing to reduce over the last weeks to zero.
- *Possible side-effects:* initial irritation of nose and throat (though this lessens with use) sneezing, runny nose, watery eyes.
- *Effectiveness:* can double success rate, especially for those heavily dependent on nicotine, smoking over 20 a day, and who have the first cigarette within 20 minutes of waking.

When NRT might not be appropriate

It is advised that you should not use NRT if you are pregnant or breast feeding. There are exceptions, but check what it says on the packet, and with a health professional first. Care should also be taken if you have heart disease, hyperthyroidism, diabetes, kidney or liver problems, gastritis or peptic ulcers or skin disorders. It makes sense to talk to your doctor or pharmacist about any existing medical conditions before self-prescribing NRT. You should not smoke while you are using it.

Zyban

A tablet containing bupropion, marketed as Zyban, helps smokers quit, probably by increasing dopamine levels in the brain. Dopamine is a neuro-transmitter associated with pleasure. We are rewarded with a dopamine hit every time we eat or have sex. Addictive drugs such as nicotine, alcohol, heroin and cocaine act on the brain in such a way that they boost dopamine levels. That is why these addictions are so hard to beat. The drug was originally marketed as an anti-depressant. It is not available over the counter, and must be obtained on a doctor's prescription.

- *Usage:* the course of treatment begins one week before the target quit date, and typically continues for around eight weeks. One tablet per day is taken for three days, and then the dosage is increased to two tablets per day. It can be used alongside NRT with your GP's approval.
- *Possible side-effects:* dry mouth and difficulty sleeping are the main side-effects (which are generally mild and often disappear after a few weeks).
- *Other considerations:* not recommended if you suffer from epilepsy or an eating disorder.
- *Effectiveness:* Zyban will at least double your chances of stopping smoking compared with no pills or placebos. One trial also suggested that the drug is more effective than nicotine patches. However, there is currently insufficient evidence to show that Zyban is more effective than NRT.

Non-nicotine products

There are a variety of non-nicotine methods also available which some quitters may find more palatable. They also have fewer side-effects.

Capsules

There are capsules made from menthyl valerate, a mild sedative to aid withdrawal, which also contain quinine, camphor and eucalyptus oil, aimed at improving breathing.

- *Usage:* 48 capsules taken over 28 days.
- *Possible side-effects:* there are no known side effects, though they should not be taken if you are pregnant.
- *Effectiveness:* there is no solid evidence that this treatment helps people to stop smoking.

Dummy cigarettes

Dummy cigarettes look like cigarettes and are tobacco flavoured, but you don't light them. They are designed to give some taste satisfaction and also give you something to do with your hands and mouth.

- *Usage:* the various brands last between one and three months, and you can use them whenever you want to.
- *Side-effects:* harmless.
- *Effectiveness:* not proven. Not recommended.

Herbal cigarettes

Herbal cigarettes are available over the counter in chemists and health food shops. You light and smoke them as you would an ordinary cigarette, the main difference being that they contain no nicotine. As with dummy cigarettes, they help if you miss the action of smoking, but it also means that you don't deal with this aspect of your habit. The idea is to replace normal cigarettes with these and then gradually give up altogether.

- *Usage:* when you feel the desire to smoke.
- *Side-effects:* although they contain no nicotine, they still include tar and carbon monoxide, both of which are very harmful. Tar contains chemicals that irritate the lungs and airways, and is a main cause of cancer. Carbon monoxide replaces oxygen in the blood, and contributes to heart disease.
- *Effectiveness:* no proven long-term benefits, and they are likely to be harmful to health for the reasons outlined above. Not recommended.

Filters

These are added to ordinary cigarettes, to cut down the amount of nicotine and tar you inhale. But many smokers simply inhale more heavily, or smoke more to compensate. These filters are similar to switching to a low-tar brand and can be counter productive.

- *Usage:* fitted to each cigarette you smoke.
- *Side-effects:* the same as for smoking.
- *Effectiveness:* not proven.

Mouthwash

A mouthwash with a special preparation containing silver acetate is available in some countries and is supposed to work by making cigarettes taste unpleasant. The product recommends you gargle with it for about 15 seconds whenever you feel a strong desire to smoke. It affects the taste of cigarettes for three to four hours, but it also adversely affects the taste of food for about half an hour.

- *Usage:* as required.
- *Side-effects:* none, but pregnant women are advised to check with the doctor before using it.
- *Effectiveness:* not clinically proven. Not recommended.

Counselling and support groups

Because smoking involves so much more than a physical addiction to nicotine, and there are behavioural and emotional implications when you make what amounts to a life style change by becoming a non-smoker, support of some description greatly increases your chances of success.

QUITLINE (0800 002200)

Our trained counsellors provide help with the often very complex reasons for smoking and the emotional factors involved in stopping. The service is free to the user, and you can use it as much as you want. Because help is offered on the phone, you don't have to travel to use it, and can access it at work as well as at home. The calls can be as long or as short as suits you, and you choose to focus on what you want to talk about. You will cover much the same ground as you would with a one-to-one counsellor, the difference being that you are likely to talk to a different person each time you phone. A study published in a medical journal in 2000 found that 22 percent of smokers who called the QUITLINE for help with quitting succeeded in stopping smoking for a year. This compares very well with quit rates for people trying to quit without any special help.

Counselling
One-to-one sessions with a counsellor can help by allowing you to explore your habit in depth, and better understand why you smoke, as well as discovering why you want to stop and what will motivate you to do so. Counselling usually starts from the premise that cigarettes meet some genuine need, and aims to help the smoker to get through what is therefore seen as a difficult experience. You will usually have to pay for this service.

Life coaching
A life coach will work with you by taking a rounded look at your life, helping you to identify pressures, professional and personal, which may be contributing to your dependency on smoking. Coaches will usually ask you to make changes in the way that you care for yourself, and encourage and support you in eliminating the elements in your life that cause you stress. Rather than tackling smoking directly, they will usually help you decide on actions to make your life happier and more relaxed so that quitting becomes easier. The main

difference from counselling is that coaching concentrates more on practical things you can do to help yourself, and a coach will expect you to take agreed actions between sessions. It is usually conducted over the phone, and you pay for sessions.

Internet support

If you have access to the internet there is now a variety of message boards, chat rooms and websites which support smokers as they try to kick the habit and stay stopped. It can be a useful forum for swapping ideas, looking at what works and what doesn't, finding out about new products as they come on the market, reading about the personal struggles of others to overcome nicotine addiction and disclosing your own personal journey. It can also be a way to make friends going through a similar experience.

Smokers' clinics

Smoking cessation groups provide much-needed mutual support, as you quit alongside other people. Some groups are run by healthcare professionals or QUITLINE counsellors, and typically involve five to eight one- or two-hour sessions. Your local doctor's surgery may run such a group. A range of local services may be available in your area to help smokers give up. For example, every health authority runs a specialist smoking cessation service. Call QUITLINE on 0800 002200 for details of your nearest service.

Research has shown that smokers are up to four times more likely to stop smoking by attending a specialist smokers' clinic than by using willpower alone. Some kind of group support together with NRT seems to work best for heavy smokers. In the future, specialist clinics will probably use Zyban as an aid to cessation.

> I had attended a 'stop smoking' group at the local health centre, because I was made to. It didn't work for any of us in the group at the time – all of us had been required to attend. But years later I remembered some of the things the health visitor leader had said and they kicked in when I was ready and able. I wrote to her then, and told her not to get disheartened if people didn't give up at once as her materials were certainly the right ones to use – in fact they were too right in some ways because smokers can't always face the real medical significance of what they are doing on top of trying to give it up as well. The reality of knowing about the damage makes you want a fag, and quick! But I date my giving up to what we did in the group.

Alternative therapies

There are several alternative therapies available for smokers who want to quit. Some claim a success rate as high as 95 per cent but be warned: all objective experts agree that any method which claims over 30 percent success rate is unlikely to be accurate. QUIT only endorses methods that have been subject to independent clinical trials. If you really believe in a method, however, your belief alone could make it work for you.

Hypnosis and hypnotherapy

Hypnosis involves you being guided into entering a state of relaxation voluntarily. During this time the practitioner will talk to you and implant ideas that are believed to help you give up. Not everyone is able to enter this relaxed state.

There are many different techniques and the number of sessions varies according to the individual practitioner. Some claim a one-hour session is sufficient for you to give up. Others offer more and longer sessions together with counselling. You can also buy self-hypnosis tapes to listen to at home. Whichever method is used, however, your own motivation is always the highest indicator of success.

Hypnotherapy is a branch of psychotherapy that uses hypnosis as a therapeutic tool. This method may involve branches of mainstream psychology, such as cognitive behavioural therapy, which helps you to change your thought patterns from those that are unhelpful or damaging. There is insufficient independent evidence to substantiate the effectiveness of hypnotherapy.

Acupuncture

Acupuncture is one of the traditional treatments from the East, with a 2000-year history. Acupuncture works by painlessly inserting needles into your body to balance energies, and to deal with specific conditions, such as nicotine craving. A qualified practitioner should also consider your life-style, diet, exercise and relaxation while tackling the specific problem. Sometimes the treatment involves inserting a staple or needle point into the ear which is left in place for about a week. Applying pressure to the staple is supposed to reduce the desire to smoke when craving occurs. If you do choose to try this method, make sure you use a practitioner who is a member of a regulatory body. There is no good evidence that acupuncture helps people to stop smoking.

Laser therapy

This is claimed to work in a similar way to acupuncture but instead of needles, a cold laser beam is directed at the sites of the traditional acupuncture points in the body. The idea is to reduce withdrawal symptoms by stimulating the body's natural painkillers – endorphins. These drop when you give up smoking so laser treatment is supposed to aid this aspect of withdrawal. Very little research has been carried out. The method has not as yet been proven and should be approached with caution.

Homeopathy

This is a system of treating conditions by taking small quantities of drugs or other substances that excite symptoms similar to that of the condition. Some remedies are supposed to work particularly on emotional and psychological states, which are presumed to help with the feelings that are churned up when you are withdrawing from smoking, such as anger and impatience, or even grieving. Other remedies work to increase the detox effect, or help you to sleep. The effectiveness has not been demonstrated for smoking cessation.

Allen Carr Method

I'd tried to give up loads of times. I finally bit the bullet and went through the torture of it using Allen Carr's book, and the wonderful idea that the less you feed your addiction the less hungry it gets. It turned out to be totally true. I put on 20 pounds but I did lose it in the end. I felt like a different person. I *am* still a different person. I cry more easily (smoking just suppressed all my feelings and when I gave up, all the pain I had felt at things in the past came down on me as if they had been waiting there all along). All I can really remember now, six years later, is the thing to do is know that once you stop you should never start again. If I had one puff now I know I would be hooked within days. It isn't worth it. I was a cigarette with a body attached to it before. People used to tell me they could not imagine me not smoking, now they say the opposite.

The Allen Carr method is delivered face-to-face at his clinic, and is also described in a series of books. It claims to be instant and permanent, and that smokers will be able to quit without using willpower or suffering from withdrawal symptoms. Some people have found that it boosts motivation and helps clarify thinking, and say that the method is very helpful. However, there is no independent clinical evidence to support his claims that over 80 percent of clients succeed after one session at his clinic. A small study carried out for Quit by St George's Hospital Medical School revealed that a figure of around 30 percent abstinence at the six-month follow-up is much more likely – that is, very similar to other face-to-face methods.

I was smoking nearly 60 a day when I went to Allen Carr's clinic, and I was sceptical. The session was very powerful, with its emphasis on the joy of being free from the addiction. I walked out feeling vulnerable – I wouldn't have cigarettes to 'protect' me anymore – and hopeful. As promised, I found stopping really easy. I had no withdrawal symptoms, even in the early days, and apart from putting on weight I had no trouble at all. Then five months later I started having the odd cigarette. I can hardly remember why. After a few weeks of secret smoking away from my girlfriend and colleagues I 'came out' as a smoker again. About a year later I went back to Allen Carr, for a session he runs for people who have relapsed. I only stopped for a few hours that time. A couple of years after that I tried again, with the original session. It just didn't move me as it had the first time, and I carried on smoking. It put me off trying the other methods people use to give up smoking. But I'll still be up for trying any magic new developments.

Conclusion

There is a great deal of money to be made out of people like you who want to stop smoking. So it's perhaps inevitable that there are a number of methods that promise much on the market. Unless there is independent evidence of efficacy, treat it with extreme caution. The best way to find out if a method is *bona fide* is to ask a trained healthcare practitioner. A practice nurse or sister, health visitor or doctor should be able to advise you. Any method that boasts an exceptionally high success-rate should be regarded with caution. If in doubt, call QUITLINE on 0800 002200 and we will tell you if a method you are considering has been independently assessed.

Even if a method has been demonstrated to be effective, this only means that it will help to increase your chances of success. The main determinant of your success, however, will still be your own internal motivation to quit.

Further help

All information was correct at the time of publication, but QUIT cannot accept any responsibility for subsequent changes.

Useful telephone numbers
All numbers beginning 0800 are free to phone

QUITLINE	0800 002200 (7 days)
QUIT	020 7388 5775
Bengali QUITLINE	0800 002244 (Mondays)
Gujerati QUITLINE	0800 002255 (Tuesdays)
Hindi QUITLINE	0800 002266 (Wednesdays)
Punjabi QUITLINE	0800 002277 (Thursdays)
Turkish/Kurdish QUITLINE	0800 002299 (Thursdays and Sundays)
Urdu QUITLINE	0800 002288 (Sundays)
Pregnancy QUITLINE	0800 169 9 169
Action on Smoking and Health (ASH)	020 7739 5902
Allen Carr Helpline	0891 664401
Asthma Helpline	0845 701 0203
British Acupuncture Council	020 8735 0400
British Association for Counselling	01788 550 899
British Heart Foundation	020 7935 0185

British Homeopathic Association	020 7935 2163
British Hypnotherapy Association	020 7723 4443
Cancer Bacup	0808 800 1234
Cancer Research Campaign	020 7224 1333
Cancerlink	0800 132 905
CQ Stop Smoking Plan	0800 092 93 92
Drinkline	0800 917 8282
Imperial Cancer Research Fund	0207 7242 0200
National Drugs Helpline	0800 776600
NHS Smoking Helpline	0800 169 0 169
Nicotinell Helpline	0800 917 3333
No Smoking Day	020 7916 8070
Samaritans	0845 790 9090
Smokeline Scotland	0800 84 84 84
Zyban Helpline	0800 1 69 70 80
0800 2 GIVEUP (Nicorette)	0800 2 44 83 87

Useful websites

www.quit.org.uk
www.ash.org.uk (Action on Smoking and Health)
www.bhf.org.uk (British Heart Foundation)
www.crc.org.uk (Cancer Research Campaign)
www.givingupsmoking.co.uk
www.healthnet.org.uk/quit
www.iquitonline.com
www.nicorette.co.uk
www.nicotinell.co.uk
www.niquitincq.co.uk
www.no-smoking-day.org.uk
www.quitnet.org
www.thetimeisright.co.uk
www.coachreferral.com (for finding a Life Coach)

Index

Action on Smoking and Health
  see ASH
acupuncture 9, 111, 175, 191–2
addiction *see* nicotine
adrenalin 29, 91
alcohol 38, 42, 53, 97, 98, 117,
  159, 184
Alexander technique 139
Allen Carr method of quitting
  192–4
aromatherapy 131, 139
ASH (Action on Smoking and
  Health) 3

blood sugar 131
body fat *see* weight
brain, effect of nicotine on
  115–16
bupropion *see* Zyban

caffeine, effects of 90, 120
camphor 185
cancer of:
  bladder 30
  breast 26
  cervix 30
  duodenum 30
  kidneys 30, 89, 183
  larynx 30
  lips 30
  mouth 30
  oesophagus 30
  pancreas 30
  stomach 30
  throat 10, 30
  womb 26
  other mentions 30, 45,
    134, 186
carbon monoxide in tobacco
  smoke 19, 29, 176, 186
children:
  susceptibility to illness 33, 135
  effects of parental smoking on
    33
cocaine 117, 184
cognitive behavioural therapy 191
cold turkey 7 *see also* withdrawal
  symptoms
concentration, loss of 119
coronary disease *see* heart and
  circulation
cot death *see*

pregnancy and
  smoking
coughing 19, 119, 120, 182
counselling and support *see*
  QUITLINE counsellors

detoxing 118, 120, 121, 156, 192
  see also withdrawal symptoms
diabetes 26, 183
diet:
  eating disorders 184 *see*
    also Zyban
  need for balanced 106, 138,
    149, 191
digestive system 89:
  constipation 90, 120
  diarrhoea 111, 120
dizziness 121
dopamine 116, 117, 184
dummy cigarettes 185

endorphins 91, 124, 192
epilepsy 184
  see also Zyban
eucalyptus oil 185
exercise:
  and breathing 49–50, 60
  and increased energy 19,
    149, 153
  as stress reducer 56, 91, 124,
    138–9, 167
  fitness and health 56, 92, 102,
    120, 134–5, 149, 156
  weight control and 24, 56, 91,
    122, 149

filters 186
fluid intake 89–90, 120–1, 131,
  139, 140, 159, 178
  see also caffeine, effects of

gall bladder 26
gangrene 30
gastritis 183
glucose sweets 131

habit, smoking as a 1, 10, 44–5,
  46, 113, 167
  strategies for quitting
    47, 48–52
headaches 111

heart and circulation:
  blood circulation 19, 30,
    89, 119
  heart disease 19–20, 25, 26, 28,
    29, 108, 134, 183, 186, 189
  high blood pressure 19, 26, 29
  oxygen supply 29–30, 31, 32,
    33, 89, 121, 186
  strokes 29–30, 108
  see also PVD (peripheral
    vascular disease)
helpline, telephone *see* QUITLINE
herbal cigarettes 185–6
heroin 45, 89, 126, 184
holistic approach 102
homeopathy 111, 112, 192
hunger 89–90, 106, 113, 121, 141
hyperthyroidism 183
hypnosis and hypnotherapy 9,
  111, 190, 191

inhalators 177, 182
internet support 189

laser therapy 192
lethargy 120, 130, 131
life coaching *see* QUITLINE
  counsellors
life and health insurance 135
low incomes, smokers on 102
  community programmes
    for 3–4

massage 139
meditation 56
meningitis 32
menthyl valerate capsules 185
metabolism 56, 90, 149
  metabolic rate 25, 121
mouth bacteria 121
mouth ulcers 121
mucus 119
myths about quitting 23–8

nasal spray 177, 182–3
National Society of Non-
  Smokers *see* QUIT
nausea 111
  see also nicotine gum; nicotine
    lozenges; nicotine tablets
neuro-transmitters *see* dopamine
nicotine:

absorption 178, 179, 180, 181, 182, 183, 184
addiction 1, 10, 45, 53, 67, 115, 116, 127, 136, 167, 174, 176, 187, 189
craving 9, 21, 38, 45, 46, 47, 48, 50, 52, 65, 91, 103, 117, 118, 170, 174, 177, 191
see also withdrawal symptoms
nicotine gum 47, 53, 57, 163–4, 177–9
nicotine lozenges 179
nicotine patches 16, 28, 39, 150, 152, 177, 180–1, 184
nicotine replacement therapy (NRT):
inappropriate use of 183
other mentions 46, 116, 164, 175, 176–83, 190
nicotine tablets 179–80
'No Smoking Day' 12, 40
NRT see nicotine replacement therapy

passive smoking 15, 33, 163
Pavlov, Ivan (Russian physiologist) see Pavlovian effect
Pavlovian effect 126
peptic ulcers 183
phlegm 120
pneumonia 31
poor concentration 113
pregnancy and smoking, effects on:
birth weight 32
breast feeding 33, 183
conception 31
growth and development 32
life expectancy 33
miscarriage 32
premature birth 32
Sudden Infant Death Syndrome (SIDS) (cot death) 30
waters breaking 32
other mentions 15–16, 31, 32, 99, 111, 124, 125, 162, 168
see also children
psoriasis 34
pulse rate 19
PVD (peripheral vascular disease) 30
see also heart and circulation

quinine 185
QUIT 1–5, 82, 148, 169, 174, 190, 193
QUITLINE (0800 002200) 1–2, 4–6, 7, 94, 140, 155, 157, 161–2, 164, 171, 189, 194
QUITLINE counsellors:

approach of 2, 4–5
life coaching and cessation groups 188–9
minority groups 4
training of 2, 5, 17
other mentions 10, 24, 38, 41, 46, 73, 86, 124, 149, 156, 164, 168, 187–8
'Quitter of the Year Award' 77, 78, 152
quitting aids, non-nicotine 185–7

reflexology 139
relapsing:
areas of vulnerability 20–1, 41, 44
coping with 20–1, 104, 129–30, 150, 151, 174
lack of motivation 17
need for support 167–8, 174
relaxation and calming techniques 56, 60, 124, 131, 139, 191
respiratory disease:
chronic bronchitis 31
emphysema 31, 45
impaired lung function 19, 30, 31, 50, 119, 140, 175
lung cancer 14, 21, 30, 108, 112
other mentions 13, 16, 19, 113, 182, 186
see also coughing
restlessness 113

sex and fertility 16, 31, 32
see also pregnancy and smoking
SIDS (Sudden Infant Death Syndrome) see pregnancy and smoking
silver acetate mouthwash 187
skin, effects of smoking on 15, 33–4, 38, 135
sleep disturbance 113, 120, 151–2, 184
see also nicotine patches
smell of smoke on:
breath 77, 111, 141, 165
clothing 15, 165, 108
hair 15
furnishings 83
smoking cessation groups 189–90
see also QUITLINE counsellors
smoking, high cost of 14–15, 77, 78, 102, 134–5
potential savings 51, 56, 64, 74, 79, 104, 151, 152, 163
social smoking 15, 64–5, 101, 122, 146
sore tongue 121
stomach ulcers see nicotine gum
stress:

caused by quitting smoking 22, 56–7, 91, 131–2
dealing with 138–40, 141, 188
smoking and coping with 11, 20, 26–8, 35, 61, 100, 101, 122–3, 137–8, 156, 159
see also exercise
strokes see heart and circulation
Sudden Infant Death Syndrome (SIDS) see pregnancy and smoking

T'ai Chi 56, 139
tar content of cigarettes 176, 186
taste and smell, sense of 19, 108, 119, 135, 164
therapies, alternative 9, 111, 112, 175, 190–4

vitamin supplements:
vitamin A 33
vitamin C 140
other mentions 131

weight:
gain 24–5, 91, 106, 108, 121–2, 137, 148, 149, 193, 194
smoking to control 11, 13
storage of body fat 25–6, 33
willpower 5, 23–4, 52, 84, 97
withdrawal symptoms, psychological and emotional:
anger and irritability 26, 27, 59–60, 91, 111, 113, 124, 125, 137, 142, 143, 144, 145, 166, 167
anxiety and nervousness 20, 27, 113
boredom 58–9, 124, 144
depression and loneliness 62–3, 113, 123, 124, 132, 144, 166
deprivation 144, 137
grieving 192
impatience 192
mood swings 124, 166, 167, 171
rebelliousness 12, 67–9, 101
resentment 160
sadness and crying 91, 123, 132, 141, 150, 166
other mentions 1, 10, 12–13, 44–5, 53–5, 174, 187
workplace, no-smoking policies in the 4

Yoga 56, 139
young smokers, 3, 11, 70–1, 73–5, 100, 134, 146, 157, 162, 163

Zyban 184, 190